The Journalism Manifesto

T0087468

The Manifesto Series

Barbie Zelizer,
Pablo J. Boczkowski and
C. W. Anderson

The Journalism
Manifesto

polity

First published in 2022 by Polity Press

Polity Press
65 Bridge Street
Cambridge CB2 1UR, UK

Polity Press
101 Station Landing
Suite 300
Medford, MA 02155, USA

ISBN-13: 978-1-5095-4263-5
ISBN-13: 978-1-5095-4264-2 (pb)

A catalogue record for this book is available from the British Library.

Library of Congress Control Number: 2021938632

Typeset in 11 on 15pt Sabon by
Cheshire Typesetting Ltd, Cuddington, Cheshire
Printed and bound in Great Britain by CPI Group (UK) Ltd, Croydon

The publisher has used its best endeavors to ensure that the URLs for external websites referred to in this book are correct and active at the time of going to press. However, the publisher has no responsibility for the websites and can make no guarantee that a site will remain live or that the content is or will remain appropriate.

Every effort has been made to trace all copyright holders, but if any have been overlooked the publisher will be pleased to include any necessary credits in any subsequent reprint or edition.

For further information on Polity, visit our website:
politybooks.com

"Listen: Billy Pilgrim has become unstuck in time."
Kurt Vonnegut, Jr., *Slaughterhouse-Five*

Contents

Acknowledgments

This book started in London, one stormy Sunday morning in late autumn of 2018, when Mary Savigar at Polity Press approached one of us with the proposal of writing a book on journalism for the new Manifesto series. A lot has happened to each of us in our personal lives, as well as to the world, between that day and when we submitted the final version of this manuscript in the spring of 2021. We alternated fascinating conversations with periods of silence. We supported each other when life got in the way of work by one of us spontaneously taking the lead when the others needed a break. We wrote and edited each other's words to the point that we could guess each other's thoughts and finish each other's sentences. We started this project animated by the diversity of our viewpoints and wrapped it up with a fusion of our ideas. We

Acknowledgments

ended up cherishing the manuscript, but even more our friendship.

Through it all, Mary, Stephanie Homer and Ellen MacDonald-Kramer at Polity Press graced us with outstanding support and unparalleled patience. We could not have hoped for a better editorial team. We are also grateful for the helpful feedback given by the anonymous reviewers solicited by Polity.

Last, but not least, this book would not exist without the countless conversations each of us has had with other scholars, practitioners, sources and members of the public over the past few decades. A lot of what we know and how we think about journalism is the outcome of these conversations. We hope the resulting text does some justice to how much each of you has taught us, and sparks new conversations in return.

1

Journalism in the Imagination and on the Ground

For much of journalism's study, the news and its newsmakers have been imagined as belonging to an institution perched in pristine isolation from its surroundings. Invoking widely used practices, oft-proclaimed values and publicly heralded standards has helped to produce and sustain a uniform and isolationist view of how journalism works. With journalism studies by and large helping to cheerlead it on, this view defends the sequestered institution of the press and its role in society while making the assumption, typically implicit but sometimes stated, that journalism's worth is unquestionable. Both impulses reveal what an exercise in unreflective quarantine from the world might look like.

This manifesto seeks to put journalism back into the world where it belongs by bringing its imagination and its ground into closer quarters with each other. We argue that, if journalism is to have a future in these unsettled and unsettling times, it must stop resting on its laurels and instead reset its connections to what lies beyond its boundaries. Journalism needs to revisit its engagement with society, rethink its priorities, rekindle relevancies gone dormant and question its default settings. If it does not, its future is surely at risk.

The disarray of institutions

In all of its guises, journalism exemplifies the shaky status of the "separate but equal" myth about institutional culture that has prevailed across most western liberal democracies of late modernity and their permutations in the Global North. Encouraging thinking about institutions in certain ways and not others, the entrenchment of that myth across time and space has delivered a view of institutions as separatist endeavors that work autonomously to achieve their aims. Though early theorists of modernity had grand and expansive visions for institutions – they would help to maintain social order, promote stability, provide authoritative guidelines for behavior, coordinate activity, uphold social structure, govern and discipline the unruly – in fact, institutions have become in many ways an irritant under the surface of the collective. One source of that irritation has been their repeated proclamations of independence from each other, uttered even as growing evidence shows how interdependent all institutional settings are and will continue to be.

This has had direct ramifications on the practical dimensions of the institutional settings that have subsequently emerged. As complex social forms that mark certain activities and relationships as appropriate and imaginable while pushing alternative options from view, institutions help to consolidate the health of collectives that they aim to support. Across all of an institution's constituent features – rules, roles, rituals, conventions and norms, among others – patterning and organization help to bind activity into a consonant whole. And yet from politics to education, the military to the market, institutions function as much in accordance with the conditions of their imagination as with the conditions on the ground. When their imaginary is activated by unnecessarily narrow positionalities, it cobbles the ensuing understanding of institutions, decouples it from everyday practices and sorely undercuts their potential.

And yet institutional imaginaries persevere, filled with often unrealistic aspirations that are multiple in number, spotless in character and misleading in impact. They include notions of identifiable and stable publics, anemic expectations in the face of challenge, a resistance to change, uniformly invoked standards of action, expertise disconnected from the communities it serves, unattainable codes of ethics and unrepresentative norms. All cater to ungrounded conditions that end up producing a state of disarray, their institutional dynamics driven by unsupported and unsustainable contours for being in the world. These attributes are fatal, for they leave efforts undone and projects abandoned midway. The recent upheavals around the world, protesting as they do the racialized, gendered and otherwise discriminatory and exclusive practices that unfortunately continue to mark social life in the twenty-first century, reflect how much challenges to the institutional order have yet to be fully grappled with. Newsrooms, too, have largely failed to come to terms with the shifts in power dynamics prompted by movements such as #BlackLivesMatter and #MeToo.

We argue that much of the turmoil and confusion around journalism, an institution that inhabits this problematic landscape, stems from the adverse effects of at least four illusions about how institutions work: autonomy, centrality, cohesion and permanence. Each has been put in place by a set of thinkers – largely white, male, high status and from the West and Global North – whose predilection for certain intellectual impulses drew a picture of institutions that reflected the aspirations they held for themselves but that fared less well in attending to a host of alternative environments in which institutional settings would take hold.

Illusion of autonomy

Most academic considerations of institutions in the liberal democracies of late modernity across the West and Global North tend to presume their autonomy. Although institutions occupy shared space – where politics, the market, education and journalism are among the forces competing for public attention from fundamentally the same vantage point – they work hard to substantiate claims of independence and distinctiveness from each other. Because the combined effect of an institution's material, moral and cultural authority keeps it separate from other institutions, aspirations of autonomy are crucial for sustaining institutional identity.

Nods to autonomy pervade much of the decision-making that occurs in institutional settings. Ethics codes, mission statements, logos and other means of positioning an institution in the world imply its autonomy. The very definition of norms, for example, as expectations of permissible and appropriate behavior, presumes that behavior unfolds within institutional boundaries, hinging desired or eschewed action on an institution's independence.

But the narrowness of this assumption becomes clear when institutional practices unravel on the ground and institutional borders reveal themselves to be both porous and unstable. Even the liberal democracies central to the received view of institutions show how institutions move in various directions when responding to crisis. For example, news organizations in Sweden and Denmark took different tacks to gender-related violence in response to the #MeToo movement, according to Askanias and Hartley: Sweden covered it extensively, framing it as a structural and systemic problem, while Denmark peppered its scant coverage with accusations of a witch-hunt against men and an overly politically correct campaign. The different responses were also echoed in the legal and political institutions of each country. The notion of autonomy, then, might deserve rethinking along lines of the give-and-take that helps to create and sustain the illusion that institutions could be autonomous while admitting that they rarely are.

We thus might want to consider what happens when an institution's dynamics have a domino effect on other institutions. As they are all part of a shared culture, each institutional setting is directly affected by what happens in adjacent ones.

Illusion of centrality

Notions of autonomy are tied to assumptions about the centrality of institutions in social life. Many theorists of institutional settings in western and global northern liberal democracies have regarded institutions as necessary for societies to function, becoming, in Raymond Williams' eyes, "the normal term for any organized element of society" (1976, 169). As Everett C. Hughes argued, "participation in the life of the community becomes increasingly a matter of participating in some way in institutional activities" (1936, 182). Sociality came to be seen as depending centrally on institutions that were woven into the fabric by which societies exist.

Societies, however, come in all shapes and sizes, and many preclude a reliance on institutions and their trappings. Societies which rely heavily on activism, for instance, such as many countries in Latin America, tend to privilege non-institutional forms of political engagement over traditional modes of interaction centered on the institution, and social movements often take on the role that institutions might play elsewhere. Countries favoring modes of collective over institutional engagement might involve different sectors in society: the often-bypassed history of Black journalism in the United States, for instance, has long celebrated activism as its journalistic mantra. Black journalism blossomed, as Sarah J. Jackson argues, despite – or, perhaps, because of – a clear distaste for activist impulses in the mainstream media.

In the best of cases, then, institutional centrality is seen not as an end in itself as much as a means of enacting and performing the shared imagined purpose of liberal democratic institutions. Amidst expectations of transparency, engagement, efficacy and fairness, institutions use mechanisms to establish a preferred social identity and to entrench the idea that they exist to better public life. Called "face-work" by Erving Goffman, these mechanisms have been seen as central to late modern societies, where they elicit trust in abstract concepts and systems and in a desired ability to work for the common good. In this, our argument parallels the one made by Steve Reese (2021), who proposes that we think of journalism as a decentralized "hybrid" institution scattered across many sites. Our diagnosis of the crisis, however, may be more dire than Reese's, and thus the institutional challenge we mount may be greater than his.

The centrality of institutions is also questionable today in many formerly stable liberal democracies, where government, religion, the military, science, the media, medicine and law are among those undergoing systemic challenges that regularly and repeatedly sideline their effectiveness and cultural authority. One such case is Hungary, whose government labored intensely to dismantle the Central European University in 2018, challenging its broad repute as one of the best universities in the region. Hungary's current state of extreme polarization, found in other illiberal democracies too, pushes back on the idea that institutions can work satisfactorily for all of society. This goes a long way in sidelining expectations of centrality.

Illusion of cohesion

Ideas of autonomy and centrality are connected to beliefs about the cohesion of institutional fields. Coming from perhaps the leading western cultural sociologist of the late nineteenth century, Émile Durkheim's famous insistence on consensus over dissensus, order over chaos, "normality" over pathology, continues to stoke many ongoing discussions of the western liberal democratic institutions of late modernity. Linked to the sociological penchant for identifiable and controllable aspects of social life, cohesion's privileging has been central to the scholarly imaginary which gives institutions shape. As Charles Taylor established more broadly of modernity's normative backdrop, "The basic normative principle is . . . that the members of society serve each other's needs, help each other, in short behave like the rational and sociable creatures they are . . . The basic point of the new normative order is the mutual respect and mutual service of the individuals who make up society" (2004, 12).

Though cohesion is often taken as a trait of societies external to institutions, the aspiration for cohesion inside of an institution presupposes that all aspects of its setting stick together in some basic way. Cohesion makes it possible for institutions to thrive on routines, predictable conventions, bureaucracy, orderly arrangements and hierarchical chains of command. When an institution's dimensions take shape in an orderly and patterned fashion, stability comes to be seen as part and parcel of institutional cohesion. Though this picture is valid at times, it does not describe the full range of behavior on the existing institutional landscape.

Rather, the received view of institutions reveals serious leakage. Democratic backsliding, for example, is now in progress in every continent of the world, unsettling democracy in locations as varied as Turkey, Poland, Zimbabwe, the United States, Russia, Cambodia and Venezuela. This suggests that, for many, cohesion and stability are a faraway dream. Additionally, many institutional settings across the Global South privilege the kind of cohesion necessary for realizing shared identity but not for accomplishing the aims consonant with the received institutional imaginary. In much of Asia and Africa, for instance, functioning for the collective becomes an integral part of identity and, when needed, resistance, with shared identity complicating and challenging the exclusive nature of settled views of sociality.

What happens to cohesion when instability, turmoil and even chaos emerge? This certainly describes much of the world today, where the uncertainty wrought by autocratic and populist governing trends, a devastating and unimaginable pandemic, a reckoning with longstanding racism and the oppression of other marginalized communities and a deepening climate emergency has shattered the illusion of cohesion. The ensuing precariousness, we argue, strikes at the heart of what institutions are even about. This uncertainty raises the question of what institutions might look like were they to be understood as settings for organizing disorder without adjacent expectations that cohesion would eventually emerge from controlled chaos.

Illusion of permanence

It is not only the autonomy, centrality and cohesion of institutions that are in doubt, but also the very idea of their permanence seems more a possibility than a given nowadays. Back in 1936, Everett C. Hughes maintained that one of the most agreed-upon dimensions of institutions was their permanence. In the largely western, liberal democratic settings that he addressed, change was expected to occur in a slow, evolutionary manner, whereby institutions would adapt and transform primarily with foresight, deliberation and caution. A central point of continuity for the Chicago School from which Hughes came, this perspective helped to install a sense that institutions would and could be, in the best of cases, stable, reliable and trustworthy. Decades later, this foundational orientation to permanence as characteristic of institutional settings remains, with Anthony Giddens affirming that "institutions by definition are the more enduring features of social life" (1984, 24).

But this perspective's limited value is made clear by current circumstances. First, multiple environments display little stability or permanence, despite the fact that institutional settings thrive inside of them. Many African and Latin American institutions, for instance, do not necessarily work from a starting point of institutional strength but instead continuously wrestle with ongoing challenges to their durability. Second, change unfolds in multiple and often unpredictable ways. Though political, military, educational and economic institutions all adjust in response to transformations around them, change is often slowed down by contradictory impulses. Change in Africa, Akin L. Mabogunje notes, is accompanied by an ambivalence about its colonialist past, producing what he calls "institutional radicalization" or "the changing of institutions from their roots" (2000, 14011).

What does this tell us? Permanence can no longer be justified as a taken for granted, tenable or even aspirational trait of institutional life. In other words, if institutions are to survive, change needs to be seen not as a possible attribute, but as an inherent one.

Journalism in institutional disarray

Taken together, these four illusions decouple institutions from their surround, and institutional disarray sets in. In journalism, the institution ends up being disconnected from the everyday realities of everyone who matters: those who practice the craft, the subjects of their stories and the audiences of their reports. This disarray illustrates how deeply the conditions on the ground diverge from those in the imagination of its practitioners, sources and audiences, and it separates the scholarly minds who willed it into existence from those challenging the exercise's partial and unrepresentative nature. Thus, the recurrent angst over whether a future exists for journalism in an era marked by dwindling profits, plummeting credibility and virulent attacks by political leaders across the ideological spectrum has helped to turn the assumptions of autonomy, centrality, cohesion and permanence into leaps of faith.

Though the autonomy of journalism from other institutions has historically varied across countries, almost universally there have been growing political entanglements between news organizations, on the one side, and officials, parties, corporate leaders and movements with all kinds of ideological orientations, on the other. The cumulative effect of this pattern has eroded the idea that journalism can – or even should – be detached from the wider institutional fabric of the society about which it reports.

Journalism in the Imagination and on the Ground

The rise and ubiquitous presence of social media in the everyday communication landscape of contemporary society have humbled news enterprises and cast serious doubts about journalism's role as the ultimate gatekeeper between events and the public. Social media have also undermined journalism's concomitant agenda-setting power. Once feared and revered, the centrality of journalism as an institution has come increasingly into question.

The fragmentation of audiences, polarization of news coverage and rise of misinformation and disinformation have dealt decisive blows to the illusion of cohesion in the media ecosystem. This illusion is reflected vividly in textbooks that describe an idealized occupational culture, one often disconnected from the actual routines of those who currently practice the trade.

Though a nod to permanence was an emblematic sentiment across the early ethnographers of newsrooms, their accompanying explanations – that such nods were little more than what Gaye Tuchman (1978) called "strategic rituals" or Herbert Gans (1979) "journalistic paraideology" – hinted early on that permanence was not certain. They also established that acts of recurrent strategic legitimation were necessarily implicated in the illusion of permanence.

Illusions and leaps of faith can only take us so far. Positioned as safeguards for journalism's relevance, they achieve, in fact, the opposite. If journalism is to survive, notions of its autonomy, centrality, cohesion and permanence need to be rethought from the core.

Institutional interfaces

This manifesto argues that journalism currently inhabits a space of dislocation, and we are running out of time to repair it. Hampered by the adverse effects of orienting toward autonomy, centrality, cohesion and permanence, journalism struggles to keep in pace with the ongoing changes around it. Because the institution is itself difficult to visualize and locate, searching for the interfaces by which journalism links to the outside world provides a way of discerning which of its parts need adjusting first.

Three such interfaces – elites, norms and audiences – play a critical role in cementing journalism's irrelevance and deepening its institutional disarray. Often misread by journalists and journalism scholars alike, they have been either reduced repeatedly to the notions of economic disruption that have occupied scholarly onlookers for decades or laundered for accommodation into journalism's imaginary and cleansed of the residue that complicates their realization.

Yet each interface provides a connector to the terrain beyond journalism: the sources from which it gets information about the events it covers, the norms by which it makes sense of this information and turns reports into stories, and the relationships it develops with the publics for whom its stories are created. Journalism draws much of its material from elites; norms help it to determine a stance on that material and organize it into a coherent story-pattern; and audiences ultimately give that material meaning by both incorporating it into their everyday lives and engaging in social and political action. If the ways of thinking we discuss here were adjusted more fully to current conditions, in one way or another, each interface might generate an opportunity to recouple journalism with the world where it belongs and reinstate its relevance.

Elites

Bill Kovach and Tom Rosenstiel observed, in their classic account *The Elements of Journalism*, that "the primary purpose of journalism is to provide citizens with the information they need to be free and self-governing" (2014 [2001], 12). The origins of much scholarship on journalism hover over this point. As far back as Walter Lippmann's *Public Opinion* in 1922, scholars and critics have attempted to reconcile the truth of the "citizen as audience" with the larger democratic hopes for the power of news, ignoring most of journalism's functioning in non-democratic societies. For the most part, the solution has been to abandon citizens for elites. Under this view, the democratic deficit of the citizenry is not all that important because democracy really functions as an elite representative system. Ordinary people are assumed to fill a plebiscitary function where they periodically hold the political system to account, but otherwise the power really lies elsewhere. What this means for journalism is that its relationship with elites and democratic representatives – as sources of information and as audiences for news – is ultimately more important than its relationship with the citizenry. The institution is decoupled from its public. Moreover, what the citizenry looks like elsewhere goes largely unnoticed.

The problem for journalism in the global northern liberal democracies of the twenty-first century is that political elites are themselves a problem. Public trust in elite systems across the board – from churches to the police – has caved. Even more ominously, elite systems seem to be irrevocably divided between a responsible centrist governance wing and almost nihilistic extremes of deliberate misgovernance. Journalists are thus increasingly forced to choose between either representing the range of important political opinions that actually exist or holding fast to their liberal foundations as democratic enablers. How does one enhance the democratic potential of an elite system in which a sizable and growing portion of the public no longer believes in liberal democracy? Although this question is primed for liberal democratic systems, it bears too upon the positionality of elites writ large. Elites do not fare well in institutional settings that are already on the decline.

Norms

Seen as prescriptions for acting as members of an institutional setting, norms constitute a potential marker of a successful institution, offering what Jeannette Colyvas and Walter Powell (2006) call its "taken-for-grantedness." When norms are in little need of articulation, discussion or adjustment, they readily and often invisibly inhabit an institution's unmarked territory, providing subtle cues about how to remain in line with assumptions of appropriate and acceptable action.

But norms energetically punctuate the environment when they are threatened, repudiated, challenged or otherwise thrown onto institutional front stages. The relevance of this to institutional disarray should be clear. For today, the taken for granted dimensions of the institution of journalism are in chaotic play, partly caused by the irrelevance of journalistic norms to current conditions. Whether it be standards of objectivity and balance in news storytelling or the decorum induced by deference and moderation, norms in current use are doing little to boost the value, sharpness or relevance of journalism as an institution and are ultimately failing the practitioners on whose behalf they have been instated.

As norms have become increasingly vacuous, they are drawing journalists back to a reality that exists more readily in history books and celebratory memoirs than in current newsrooms. Though they have been widely invoked as instrumental to the values, standards and practices of those inhabiting current liberal democratic institutions, by and large they fuel an aspirational picture of journalism that deviates starkly from its realities, both for those within settings close to the received view of institutions and for those denied attention by that view. In other words, a decoupling of institutional norms and journalistic practices needs to be addressed so that practices can be recognized and assessed on their own merits.

Audiences

The idealized version of the audiences of journalism has been defined by two traits: their practices and preferences have been assumed, and their existence has been taken for granted. Back in the day, journalists assumed – or at least behaved consistently with the assumption – that their audiences were significantly interested in public affairs reporting and appreciated both the results of that reporting and the journalistic values that led to it. Audiences too were largely taken for granted: they were always going to be there, reading a newspaper, listening to a radio newscast or watching television news.

Yet, if the first quarter-century of digital news has taught us anything, it is that the audiences for news can no longer be taken for granted. The emergence of the commercial web first, and the rise of mobile communication and social media later, are tied to a massive exodus from the news to other types of content, producing all sorts of institutional disarray. The assumed nature of practices and preferences among journalists is tied, too, to a second transformation: the shift from assumed to known audiences. Every audience practice in the digital space leaves a trace, and with it ensues knowledge accessible by journalists and their employers. That knowledge reveals that the audience preference for public affairs news is only occasionally consistent with journalistic practice. Perhaps reporters and editors always knew this. But, if so, they certainly kept acting as if it were not true. Meanwhile, the rise of social media has amplified the voices of audiences, who share serious doubts about the actual practices of contemporary journalism.

The odd circumstance of assumptions being further entrenched as they involve journalistic practices and preferences, and less entrenched when it comes to audiences, underscores how out-of-touch journalistic worldviews have been toward the publics they are supposed to serve. The institution comes undone, raising the important question of how to reinstate the integral centrality of audiences without depleting journalistic function altogether.

Conclusion

What does all of this tell us? Journalism today faces receding social, political and cultural relevance, in the best case, and extinction, in the worst. Despite an unparalleled degree of technical and data sophistication, and audiences that are in some cases the largest in history, journalism is less relevant and important than it ought to be and thinks it is. It is also more relevant and important to regaining a meaningful sense of collective life in the twenty-first century. Because journalism has paid so little heed to the upending that has occurred around elites, norms and audiences, these disconnects undermine its ability to function in any kind of sustainable fashion. Before it is too late and journalism as we know it vanishes into thin air, we need to rethink and reimagine the environment in which journalism resides so as to better envision a more productive link to the world around it. In other words, we need to recouple the conditions in the imagination with the conditions on the ground.

We see two options in journalism's trajectory toward recoupling – a reformist path or a revolutionary path. Each path figures centrally in the chapters that follow and is addressed directly in the conclusion. One path expands the margins of acceptable action; the other unwinds in territory otherwise untraveled. Either path, we argue, would be better than carrying on in today's rapidly shifting world as if nothing in it could ever change. In other words, inaction or the maintenance of the status quo is no longer a viable option.

Neither path is a cure-all, nor a set of recipes for best practices. But they are blueprints toward a renewed future. In hoping for a future in which journalism showcases the voices, perspectives and experiences of the many who have been historically relegated to the narratives of the few, this manifesto charts a way for journalism to begin grappling with the importance of its own relevance for those variously marginalized by a now-fading golden age of news.

2

Elites

At the height of the first impeachment proceedings against former United States President Donald Trump, the *New York Times* ran a story titled "How the State Dept.'s Dissenters Incited a Revolt, Then a Rallying Cry." Penned before the public testimony of a series of career officials who called for Trump's impeachment, it noted that:

> Rarely has the State Department, often seen as a staid pillar of the establishment, been the center of a revolt against a president and his top appointees. But as a parade of department officials has recounted to lawmakers how policy was hijacked by partisan politics, many career diplomats say they have been inspired by their colleagues' willingness to stand up to far more powerful voices after nearly three years of being ignored or disparaged by Mr.

Trump and those he has chosen to lead the department. (Crowley et al., 2019, n.p.)

This story, like many other news reports written
during the Trump presidency, displays a process
we call the crack up of the elites. By this, we refer
to the decomposition of a relatively coherent
system of elite governance, one which journalists
have traditionally used to index their information
gathering. Under pressure from both the rise of
anti-liberal populist parties and the increasing centrality of social media in the formal and informal
mechanisms of political communication, the elite
system that once powered journalistic operations in
liberal democratic regimes has turned against itself.
The crack up of the elites introduces a wedge that
increasingly decouples governance in the imagination from governance on the ground.

We start with a recent example from the United
States, and devote considerable attention to this
country and liberal democracies in general, not
because what transpires inside their borders automatically applies to other nations. Rather, the
emphasis on these national settings in practitioner
and scholarly circles – largely due to current patterns of global economic and political power, and
the rather bombastic and highly public nature of

press–politics relationships during the Trump administration – makes particularly visible key dynamics that are central to the crack up of the elites and that often leak into other national contexts.

The crack up of the elites

The crack up of the elites creates critical procedural problems for high-level public affairs reporting that are exacerbated and complicated by a normative impasse: the anti-liberal tendencies of new elites in once-staid liberal democracies expose the underlying and unexpressed liberalism of most of the political media, forcing them to choose between their values and what they see as their duty to report about those in positions of political power. We see this clearly above in the *New York Times*, but it has been repeatedly evident across news coverage of not only the Trump presidency but also the regimes of many once-liberal democracies across the Global North. It highlights a major degradation of journalism's default setting, in which the conditions on the ground sorely undercut the conditions of the imagination. Reporting on the State Department and the first Trump impeachment proceedings resembled the coverage of political machinations in non-US autocratic countries more than the centrist, understated and unproblematized articulation of the lifetime bureaucrats of Foggy Bottom. Though that articulation had long characterized the *Times* and other consonant media, it is clear that it now falls way short of the mark.

How should journalism respond to this challenge? We argue that journalism in the United States and in countries facing similar crossroads will have to decide whether it has learned either a reformist lesson or a revolutionary lesson from the past few years. Both would represent a major change, though they signal a difference of degree and, perhaps, of kind. If journalism has learned a reformist lesson from the crack up of the elites, it will see its mission as having largely been successful: the republic did not collapse, norms were (barely) upheld and journalism outed itself as having a value system – a liberal one. In the United States, for instance, to the degree that the Republican Party would still try to overturn elections and subvert liberal democratic norms, journalism would remain opposed to such action. If journalism has learned a revolutionary lesson, however, it will have concluded that it should always be opposed to political elites, regardless of political orientation, and that this oppositional stance also needs to embrace marginalized and oppressed social groups: women, persons of color, ethnic groups, LGBTQIA people and so on, in a way that would engage in what we would claim to be a fuller reckoning with journalism's exclusions.

Why trust declines when elites crack up

Much of journalism's downward trajectory stems from an inert understanding of elites: who they are, whom they exclude, what they are expected to do and how they operate in practice. Though journalism scholars have long tried to unpack the contours of what is meant by elites and how they might function in fuller consonance with the aspired workings of democracies – especially of the western or global northern liberal tradition – they chart incisive, if contradictory, pathways to understanding the dwindling stature of elites. Equally important, they help to explain with alarming alacrity – if for no other reason than that they should have secured more attention – what the degrees of distrust and political dysfunction increasingly surrounding elites do to journalism in beleaguered democracies around the world.

Journalism has critiqued elites, but it has needed them, too. Across the globe, this balance is struck differently, both in rhetoric and in practice. Under a populist communication regime, the kind that was typical of the so-called socialist democracies of Eastern Europe up through the 1980s, the people and a segment of the elites were fused, where allegiance to one did not imply unfaithfulness to the other. In China, journalism often singles out particular factions of the elite for criticism, following the guidance of a party state intent on bolstering its own power. In the United States and parts of Europe, the people are meant to be wary and suspicious of elites, despite the fact that journalism itself has become largely an elite occupation and is reliant on elite input for scoops and tidbits of information.

In essence, mainstream journalism about public affairs has been driven largely by elites, written by elites and consumed by elites. The problem for journalism in the twenty-first century is that the political elites of global northern liberal democracies are quite problematic. The public no longer trusts a multitude of elite institutions, from religion to medicine to the army, not to mention journalists and politicians. Even more worrisome, elites seem split between "responsible" elites and nihilistic, populist leaders. Which part of the system should journalists listen to? How can journalists enhance the democratic potential of an elite system in which a large part of the public no longer believes in democracy?

The dissolution of trust is particularly dire for the relevance of expertise in journalism, because it is difficult to imagine a return to trust once it is diminished. And, in fact, increments of the dynamics surrounding the intersection of trust, expertise and elites in diminished democracies remain fuzzy wherever they are present. How much expertise is necessary to sustain trust? What part might elites play in its maintenance across irreconcilable circumstances? What roles does journalism play in response? What role can we even expect it to play? Despite strong and important national and regional differences, global patterns of news trust are not promising. According to the 2020 Reuters Institute's Digital News Report:

> less than four in ten (38%) [of respondents across all surveyed countries] said they trust most news most of the time – a fall of four percentage points from 2019. Less than half (46%) said they trust the news they use themselves. Political polarization linked to rising uncertainty seems to have undermined trust in public broadcasters in particular, which are losing support from political partisans from both the right and the left. (Newman, 2020)

Although levels of journalistic trust vary widely across the countries surveyed (with the highest rate of trust demonstrated by the Finns at 56 percent and the lowest by South Koreans at 21 percent), the 2020 report documents a general decline of trust in journalism across a number of countries since 2019. One pattern that emerges is a connection between increasing degrees of partisanship and the decline of trust in news, alongside an emphasis that generalized questions of trust are inseparable from larger questions about how different communities and countries understand journalism's purpose. In other words, while high levels of political partisanship may help to drive the decline of audience trust in news, these trends are also filtered through larger overarching understandings of the role that journalism is supposed to play. One can imagine that different normative hopes for the media would sharply distinguish different attitudes toward journalism.

All of this suggests that, in many countries around the world, the decline of trust in news is inseparable from the larger decline of trust in expert institutions in general. It rears its head particularly when the government and its associated culture of elite governance are involved.

The crack up of responsibility

Given this seemingly unstoppable collapse of trust in journalism in many parts of the world, we might hope that elites would adopt coherent positions to counteract the intensification of anti-centrifugal forces. But the opposite has happened. Recall the earlier *New York Times* story. Its tale of a fracturing establishment is one example of a larger circumstance making itself visible across the spectrum of events relying on expert intervention. Because that expert intervention is no longer possible, we argue that this tendency toward institutional decomposition is revealing itself vividly across many institutions – but especially journalism. And it is happening not only in the United States, but also in dwindling democratic governments worldwide.

All of this raises a fundamental question: If elites can no longer be counted on to "act responsibly," should journalists listen to elites at all? And if not elites, what should take their place?

At the dawn of the twentieth century, Walter Lippmann mounted a normative argument for what he called an "intelligence bureau" – an institution that could ease the impossible intellectual burden of modern democratic governance by allowing experts a greater latitude of control over public affairs. "The purpose" of such a bureau, he wrote:

> is not to burden every citizen with expert opinions on all questions, but to push that burden away from him towards the responsible administrator. An intelligence system has value, of course, as a source of general information, and as a check on the daily press. But that is secondary. Its real use is as an aid to representative government and administration both in politics and industry. The demand for the assistance of expert reporters in the shape of accountants, statisticians, secretariats, and the like, comes not from the public, but from men doing public business, who can no longer do it by rule of thumb. It is in origin and in ideal an instrument for doing public business better, rather than an instrument for knowing better how badly public business is done. (1922, 399)

Six decades later, in his classic 1973 account of the "'structured communication' of events," Stuart Hall described the uneasy relationship between elites, experts and "public forms communication," such as journalism and broadcast television in democracies: "there are few systems in which the definitions of the powerful pass, without any qualification or modification or challenge ... The connections which the media form with the elites of power are extremely complex, and contradictions – of interest, outlook, and interpretation – frequently arise between them" (1973, 18–19).

Lippmann and Hall addressed the same problem, but from diametrically opposed points of view. For Lippmann, the alignment with elites serves democracy in a roundabout way. Ordinary citizens only occasionally govern, and even less frequently have any idea what is happening in the realm of public affairs. By establishing intelligence bureaus – what we might call today the bureaucratic apparatus of government – elites not only allow journalism to occasionally produce better reporting but, even more essentially, allow representative government to function. Good journalism might even improve the quality of governance insofar as it allows public information to be fed back into the political establishment and the intelligence bureaus themselves, creating a virtuous circle of elite information. Though such a scheme appears to offer a tight model of information relay for the public good, the degree to which everyone other than elites is left out should give pause. For Hall, journalism fails its democratic function by drawing too much of its coverage from the routines and points of view of elite sources. He saw this tendency in the press to be both a political failure and a mechanism for entrenching hegemony and elite interests.

And yet, for most of the twentieth century, the "Lippmannian" solution – elite journalism as an elite activity, produced by elites and ultimately for elites – has been seen as a dominant option for understanding the role of journalism in democracy, even if it does not fully reflect the ideas and interests of those outside spheres of political power. If, as this manifesto argues, audience preferences do not necessarily encourage the production of quality journalism through market means, and if audiences are becoming increasingly quantified, segmented and disengaged from public affairs news, then high-level democracy-enhancing journalism is produced by appealing to the one audience segment that is most likely both to consume and to pay for it – namely, the elites. This is certainly not the understanding of democracy advanced by Stuart Hall, nor is it even the understanding of democracy advanced by many political theorists or journalists.

But it is not an orphan perspective within the democratic tradition, as the example of Lippmann shows. Whether or not it is a normative good, this perception is a fairly accurate description of the way market-aligned journalism has tended to function in western and global northern liberal democracies, where the surest path to economic and professional success in newsrooms across the twentieth century has been to segment audiences by education, class, race and taste preferences, while maintaining a belief that this market segment represents the public in some meaningful sense. The virtuous circle connecting elite sources of information, high-level informative journalism and elite audiences could be given a democratic gloss under a Lippmannian framework. If elites were needed for democracy to function, then the problems with public forms of communication identified by Stuart Hall would perhaps be less of a concern.

One major trouble with this solution – regardless of its degree of democratic viability – stems from the fact that we live in a world with low levels of trust in elites and experts. That trend is worsening. Journalism's functioning is premised on a relationship between the political and cultural elite – those who know what is "really happening" – and the ordinary people who use insider information to make informed political decisions. Elites, however, are seen as bankrupt by most citizens of liberal democracies across the Global North and South. They are also divided amongst themselves and increasingly unable to function as a coherent body of interests.

The Journalism Manifesto

Indexing and the spheres of political discourse

One way to theorize some of the conceptual and normative difficulties posed by changes in the journalism–elite relationship is to discuss how this relationship has been formulated through two key concepts within political communication: W. Lance Bennett's idea of journalistic indexing, and Daniel Hallin's notion of the spheres of political discourse. Both concepts are problematized on empirical and conceptual grounds by changes in elite behavior and journalistic relationships, and both radically challenge the traditional understanding of journalism's relationship with democracy.

The notion of indexing captures the fact that journalistic coverage of events depends more on the agreement or disagreement of elites than on the general contours of public opinion. In his foundational article elaborating the concept, Bennett analyzed four years of *New York Times* coverage of Nicaragua, from 1983 until 1986, and demonstrated a sharp difference between the dimensions of institutional debate with regard to American military intervention in that country – generally pro-intervention, with a substantial minority of Congress disagreeing – and the suspicion of military action voiced by the majority of the American public. More than three-quarters of the voices represented in more than 2,000 *New York Times* stories belonged to governmental officials. To the degree that multiple perspectives were represented in the coverage of Nicaragua, they were keyed – or indexed – to voices already in government. When internal governmental opposition to presidential policies faded, negative coverage of those policies faded as well. As Bennett concluded, "the evidence suggests that *Times* coverage of Nicaragua was cued by Congress, not by the paper's own political agenda or by a sense of 'adversarial journalism'" (1990, 121).

But how do we reconcile this with the two trends in elite politics that we identified earlier: a rising lack of trust in experts, and the increasing dysfunction of inter-elite politics? And how do these trends affect Bennett's concept of journalistic indexing? In some ways, Bennett foreshadowed current circumstances: "The 'new professionalism' of the press would seem to operate on the assumption that 'the system works,' despite any evidence to the contrary, and that the 'responsible press' keeps its criticisms within the bounds of institutional debate, however narrow or distorted those bounds may become" (1990, 121).

Yet already by 1990, the system was not working, with differences uncovered in indexing journalistic coverage to elite opinion and the expert system seen – even then – as obscuring the diversity of public opinion. The assumption that "the system works" was difficult to sustain in 1990. It is an impossible illusion now.

The indexing of journalistic coverage to elite cleavages has further ramifications, ones that in particular unsettle objectivity's reification of itself as journalistic common sense. Hallin's (1986) notion of the spheres of political discourse helps to explain these connections. According to him, journalists in the United States assume that social or political problems can be understood as occupying one of three spheres: consensus, in which controversy is assumed by reporters to be absent – e.g., capitalism is a good thing; legitimate controversy – e.g., debates over income tax policy and economic growth; or deviance – e.g., the atheism of a major party candidate for president. Journalistic behavior changes depending on the sphere in which a topic being reported falls. What journalists, and the public, assume to be the journalistic default – strict and studied neutrality, with both sides of an issue given equal weight in news reporting – is really only operational within the sphere of legitimate controversy. In the other two spheres, only one side of an issue exists, and thus journalists need not balance their coverage in quite the same way.

Combining Bennett's concept of indexing with Hallin's idea of the three spheres of political discourse sheds new light on the problematic relationship between elites and journalism. On the one hand, only if a topic inhabits the sphere of legitimate controversy do elites need to do their balancing work, where both sides can be given equal space to assert their views. On the other hand, changes in elite opinions can alter the manner in which public controversies are understood as either legitimate or deviant, in turn affecting journalistic willingness to publish multiple views on a particular topic. In government and activist circles, politically attuned and politically active individuals tend to focus on how the topics they care about move across various spheres. Elite understandings help to reinforce the migration of a political topic from one sphere to another, and in so doing suggest alternative pathways of interpretive action for journalists.

Changes in the sphere of consensus are not an unalloyed good thing, however. Particular fringe political positions use these shifts to become mainstream, in part because of elite reinforcement. In short, if elites grow increasingly extremist, fragmented or alienated from the public, journalism's estimates of what constitutes a legitimate controversy worthy of balanced and objective coverage become highly unstable. This is one of the factors driving the breakdown in many forms of elite journalism across the Global North and South.

Examples of this abound. Consider the erosion of democratic values and practices that characterized the early days of the now heavily autocratic regimes of Bolsonaro in Brazil, Orbán in Hungary or Erdogan in Turkey. Each presented clear challenges to journalists' ability to distinguish between legitimate and illegitimate controversy, thereby restricting the relevance of experts in the exercise of journalistic assessment. Without the reliable cues by which journalists have learned to recognize the movement of topics across spheres, how can they be expected to chart their own coverage in response? Consider again Bennett's observation, offered 30 years ago, that journalism's new professionalism operates as if the system works, despite having little or no evidence for this. If, increasingly, the system does not work and the decoupling of the expectations of elites from their actual practices on the ground becomes obvious to all, fatal degrees of tension are not far off. And when journalists fail to adjust their practices in response, tension mushrooms into full-blown crisis, channeling the unfortunate truism that you cannot teach an old dog new tricks, regardless of how much they are needed.

Conclusion

Democratic pretensions aside, we have argued here that much journalism in the West and Global North – and, by extension, often much of the Global South – is an elite activity: reported by journalistic elites, drawing on elite sources and, much of the time, specifically designated for the kind of elite audience that actually has the resources and inclination to care about politics. While many democratic theorists have looked askance at this fact, we have also sought to highlight the ways in which under a republican theory of government such a state of affairs is not entirely incompatible for democracy. Even under this scenario of reduced democratic expectations, journalism has clearly run aground.

The crack up of the elites forces journalism into a moment of reckoning, as Candis Callison and Mary Lynn Young have so aptly put it. There is little doubt that journalism has changed in recent years, and that these changes have had as much to do with shifting political and social currents as they have with technological developments. In the

United States, in particular, journalism has become more comfortable taking an oppositional stance to power, calling out known falsehoods and generally adhering to liberal principles. The big question is: What happens next? Will journalism expect a return to normalcy now that Trump has been defeated in the United States and there may be a receding authoritarian tide in Europe? Or will it begin to see itself as a defender of liberal ideas, one that stands up to attempts by elites to overthrow democracy, no matter who those elites might be? Or, finally, will journalism begin to question its reliance on elites more broadly and understand that the oppressed – women, persons of color, ethnic groups, LGBTQIA people and others – have never been well served by an elite-oriented journalism, even one that embraces liberal norms? Can journalism afford to carry on as if nothing has changed or will it adopt either a reformist or revolutionary path moving forward?

3

Norms

In 1986, a somewhat junior cultural sociologist in
the United States, ten years after receiving her doc-
torate, wrote an academic article comparing culture
to a toolkit. The piece, which contested the long-
held idea that culture is produced by internalizing
norms, likened it instead to a set of beliefs, habits,
symbols, skills, rituals and stories that people
choose to invoke strategically from multiple possible courses of action. Titled "Culture in Action:
Symbols and Strategies," it became a leading article
for the then-burgeoning area of cultural sociology,
earning its author – Ann Swidler – awards and
remaining one of the most widely cited articles in
sociology. "What endures," wrote Swidler (1986,
276), "is *the way action is organized*, not its ends."
Culture, she suggested, exists to ensure that devices
like norms need not be looked at as universal,

unilateral or unidimensional, but as options that people select in accordance with their best interests.

Still, 35 years later, we wrestle with the very premises about norms that Swidler sought to overturn. For as long as journalism has been with us, some notion of its supposedly universal, unilateral and unidimensional normative character has driven our understanding of how the news works. Norms – seen here as shared aspirational cues for occupational behavior – provide a central way of guiding journalists toward their collectivity, but they are thought to do so in decidedly flattened ways.

We argue, however, that norms, as widely understood and acted upon, miss the mark and misalign journalism's current state of occupational identity and are so entrenched that they undermine the institution's ability to function. This has added significance in today's unsettled times, when the very *raison d'être* of norms – to keep journalists focused on their supposedly better sense of selves – is rendered problematic by the relentless challenges obstructing journalism in multiple locations around the world. The normative conditions of the imagination, in other words, have been increasingly decoupled from the emerging pragmatic toolkits that journalists utilize on the ground.

Norms

Why norms?

Anyone who has looked to popular culture to tell them about the news can easily recall scenes of journalists bemoaning their shared fate as hacks while celebrating some version of normative splendor. Timothy Crouse's landmark book, *The Boys on the Bus*, was heralded as a turn-taking moment for understanding the raucous nature of pack journalism in 1973, but it simultaneously exposed how poorly journalists fared, showing little initiative when under pressure. In fact, collectivity and normativity have been hard to pry apart. Asserting a shared existence in places and at times that should matter to journalists facing the unpredictable and often uncontrollable odds of newswork, norms give individuals a reason to come together. They promise help in overcoming challenges by repairing to an aspirational vision of collective behavior and the individual's assured placement therein.

Sociological in origin, the term "norms" has popular resonance, largely as a stand-in for the oughts of collective behavior. Given its reliance on prescription, direction and injunction, the term was developed by the leading scholars of the time – largely white, male, high-status scholars who used their authoritative perches to come up with a recipe for how people ought to behave in the western liberal democracies of late modernity. Émile Durkheim was among the first to argue that norms were so important that their absence would cobble social exchange and result in anomie, prompting him to classify norms as social facts instrumental for society regardless of character, size, context, relevance or individual sentiment. His insights led other theorists such as Max Weber and Talcott Parsons to codify norms as a necessary lodestone of sociological thinking, positioning them at the heart of the social order central to understandings of collective life. For these scholars, the collective was an entity to be sustained by shared cues of appropriate and aspirational behavior. Left out of the picture was most of what complicated and prevented its realization. From the beginning, then, norms brought with them a no-can-do dimension that was critiqued by some, but nonetheless resided centrally in the normative imaginary.

Norms affect us in multiple ways: they can be implicit or explicit, broad or narrow, internally accommodated or externally sanctioned, informal or formal, direct or indirect, assumed or articulated, obligatory or optional, universal or discretionary. Building upon the longstanding scholarly juxtaposition of structure and agency, the entrenchment of norms as finding aids to group formation requires structures that can facilitate meaningful exchange between individuals. Because norms are expected to elevate what people do in tandem, moving from abstract, aspirational concepts – freedom of expression, balance, fairness – to performative enactments that people opt for when engaging socially, social life relies on the ability to share meaningful norms.

Despite their rich and wide-ranging potential, however, the deep attraction of norms falls short when they fail to deliver behavior matching their aspirational claims. Specifically, some of the messiness relevant to normative development not fully addressed by early classical scholars continues to challenge the aspirations they fixed in place. When norms are accompanied by censure and censorship, imprisonment, murder and risks to one's livelihood, they lose their benign character. The type and tenor of collectivity necessary for norms to flourish can be hard to identify, locate or accomplish. How does one behave normatively in good faith when other members of a shared collective willfully impugn, ridicule and suspend norms at will?

Across the settings most central to this imaginary, the challenges to norms have not gone unnoticed. Implicit in the wedding of ideal and typical attributes of action, norms necessarily wrestle with the question of how much aspiration is necessary to guide behavior. We argue that the answer has not been easy to find. Because norms are not as well equipped as they might be to deal with the unpredictable, surprising or serendipitous occurrence that regularly colors daily life, scholars over the years have tried to complicate their received view, pivoting them as much toward case-based ground conditions as toward the lofty notions that house aspiration.

But because the repair to ideal types tends to entrench itself most stridently in times of instability or crisis, rather than accommodate the everyday messiness of arrangements on the ground, the nod to aspiration runs rampant, nonetheless. When used to justify consensus, norms provide a way of muting or muffling conflict and contention while reducing the maneuvering space for individuality, agency and change. Though norms must be shared to exist, the collectivity they generate is almost always experienced unevenly. This is because the exercise of power is unequal by definition, making the ensuing collective less equitable than assumed and providing misguided cues as to what coming together means, entails and counts for, and for whom. These challenges are currently manifold in the western and global northern liberal democracies at the heart of the received view of norms, but they exist also across the range of illiberal practices and non-democratic regimes elsewhere – all of which were typically left out of the picture drawn by classical social theorists.

No surprise, then, that norms have not been as effective as we might think. At best, they orient to the routine and predictable, labeling singularity as deviant and promoting partial and unrepresentative collectivity. Though claiming to be good for all, they pay heed only to some and only in certain ways. Acting like what John Searle (1964) calls "constitutive rules," norms act as if they represent true conditions rather than admit the strategic nature of their construction, creating and defining new forms of behavior even if that behavior is only directed at and valued by certain actors within a setting.

What norms offer institutions

Institutions, which Tim Hallett and Marc Ventresca describe as "broad structures of meaning that are taken-for-granted and organize activity" (2006, 214), play a central role in the uneven spread of norms across collectives. Institutions help to entrench norms, which in turn act as an institution's central organizing principle. Norms reinsert social interaction into institutional settings, where they tend to be shared while caring little for explicit or implicit boundaries. This means that a norm's successful adoption requires some degree of agreement across institutions, all but ensuring both that institutional settings cater to the lowest common denominator of possibilities and that they pay little attention to what is left by the wayside.

We see this repeatedly in journalism. Consider, for example, the simple assumption that journalists could and should come together via the oughts of their behavior. This embeds telling suppositions about collective life, some of which Herbert Gans noticed as driving journalism nearly four decades ago: that it is orderly, predictable and manageable; proceeds on the basis of agreement and consensus; promotes conformity and sameness; sustains a stable set of contours; and is desired by the people it involves. Such premises characterize not only journalism but most institutions in liberal democratic regimes that regulate collective life. Yet none of these premises is a sure bet, as we are seeing in societal arrangements worldwide: intensifying social and political repression in Belarus, Azerbaijan and other formerly democratic regimes newly crippled by illiberalism and authoritarianism;

the entrenchment of structural violence associated with racism, sexism, xenophobia, homophobia and settler-colonialism across continents; the renewal of populism; and the rise of hate crimes everywhere.

Reporters and editors are often on the dark receiving end of such endeavors, constrained when the normative aspirations of collectives fall short. When journalists in India were faced with the unexpected shut-down of news organizations criticizing Hindu violence against Muslims, officials referenced "a responsible freedom" as a necessary precondition for press autonomy. In 2020, when Filipino officials convicted celebrated journalist Maria Ressa "for an article she did not write, edit, or supervise, of a crime that hadn't even existed when the story was published," the judge admonished Ressa that "to be free is not merely to cast off one's chains but to live in a way that respects and enhances the freedom of others." This is "how democracy dies in the 21st century," intoned Sheila Coronel in *The Atlantic*, "just the steady drip, drip, drip of the erosion of democratic norms, the corruption of institutions, and the cowardly compromises of decision makers in courts and congresses" (2020, n.p.).

Even the popular idea that journalists are impassively and uniformly socialized into normative behavior – "rewarded for conformity [and] punished for deviance" in Raewyn Connell's words (2002, 28) – has its limits. Were that even primarily the case, there would be little evidence of normative inertia, dissonance, protest or failure in newsrooms. Instead, the violence that has been a given in the lives of too many journalists around the globe suggests otherwise, demonstrating that a uniform response to normative convention is far more complicated than simple assumptions of voluntary compliance. Routine institutional functioning often reproduces norms by quiet force or even dictate, without much socialization taking place and without accommodating the granularity central to collectives.

Different journalistic norms also arise in different locations, even if they have not made inroads into the received view of normativity. Norms associated with anticolonialism or antiracism, for example, are widespread in the Global South but surface infrequently elsewhere. And although Georg Simmel established how inconsistent norms promote idiosyncratic behavior, norms need to reflect at the very least an approximated range of aspirations in the people to whom they are being applied. During South Africa's transition from apartheid to democracy, journalists adopted what Herman Wasserman labels a "middle class perspective on news events," despite the fact that the country's poor remained as disenfranchised by neoliberal arrangements as they had been under apartheid (2018, 81).

Norms also ride on an uneasy and ever-changing platform of recognition, challenging the institution's reliance on them. This includes a growing list of journalistic norms that were set in place long ago to address conditions that were then unrepresentative and now no longer exist. The insistence, for example, that journalism everywhere tries to be about truth, accountability and social justice is not universally applicable. As Cherian George demonstrates, when the Singaporean government changes the contours of permissible discussion of religion and race in the news, an insistence on truth becomes an enterprise that requires self-conscious and often perilous navigation.

Finally, consider the widespread belief that normative aspiration helps journalism to service the public, entrenching an understanding that the institutions of liberal democratic regimes represent the people whom they serve. While the idea that institutional actors freely take action with collective benefit in mind helps to create an expectation that institutions like journalism are capable of working for the public good, key events of recent years – from #BLM and #MeToo to COVID-19 – reveal how unsubstantiated that assumption is.

Norms of equality and colorblindness that exist in some newsrooms discourage and stifle the talk about race necessary to parse out racial inequities. At the same time, a tough approach to newswork that insists journalists "put work first" and cover the news regardless of risk silences and marginalizes women, a status exacerbated by widespread sexual harassment. The invisibility of indigenous peoples – across news management, production and coverage – underscores the deep entrenchment of settler-colonialism around the world in the locales that make the news. Every step that the imagined community of journalists takes toward inclusion is accompanied by a backdrop that continues to foster exclusion. The result is that the public served by journalism is always a sliver of the public that exists.

Recent scholarship drives home the point that all of this has long been the case in newsrooms, even if it has not been given sufficient scholarly attention. Scholars – such as Sarah J. Jackson and Catherine R. Squires on race, Candis Callison and Mary Lynn Young on indigeneity – demonstrate the ills that accompany journalism's poorly defined collectivity when it is normatively anchored. Though normativity sustains the illusion that all newswork orients to a shared purpose, it also engenders racism, sexism and misogyny, class bias, xenophobia, homophobia, settler-colonialism and other forms of oppression as a regular part of newsroom culture. Worse yet, the unremarked presence of an erroneous imagined community of journalists that bears little reflection to reality shapes coverage itself, generating representations that are at best skewed and stereotypical, at worst racist, homophobic, misogynist and elitist. Is it any surprise, then, that journalism, like other institutions, is far from stable, consensual or orderly or that it displays normative inconsistency?

Norms of journalism

Set in place in conjunction with a particular notion of journalists as professionals in the western liberal democracies of late modernity, many of journalism's occupational norms are tied to that moment. This renders them an untenable, or at best irrelevant, set of cues for understanding journalistic behavior in settings not accounted for in their original formulation. Most accounts date these conditions and timing to the rise of a western professional model of newsmaking in the late nineteenth and early twentieth centuries, alternating between political and economic explanations for its emergence: a history of liberal societies repelling authoritarianism versus one of market forces and class reconfiguration driving the need for a stance of public-mindedness and neutrality. As an ideological construct, professionalism positioned journalists as fair and balanced facilitators of deliberation and gatekeepers of the news. Though the ensuing idea of "professional" lacked definition, according to Silvio Waisbord, due to its "constant blending of occupational and normative" dimensions (2013, 6), it nonetheless offered what John Nerone sees as a "brokered settlement among three interested parties: news workers, media owners and the public" (2012, 450). Setting in place occupational standards by which journalists could sidestep bias in an organized approach to newswork, the idea of professional journalists took flight despite emergent and often contradictory ground conditions. The establishment of norms played a key role alongside other projects relevant to the project of professionalization, such as codes of ethics, trade publications and journalism schools.

Complicating this account, however, is a slew of conditions that normative thinking often minimizes or sidesteps. Claudia Mellado outlines many of them:

diverse types of authoritarianism, troubled paths towards democratization, a history of colonization (hence resemblance of press and media systems devised by imperialist powers), widespread anti-press and societal violence, weak rule of law, social/racial tensions, elite-oriented presses, limited press freedom and access to information, widespread corruption, collusive press–state relations, or concentrated property of news media. (2020, 12)

Scholars have not watched idly while the pristine side of normative ideals continues to entrench itself. Mark Deuze, for instance, argues for an occupational liquidity that forces a readjustment of the ratio between the ideal and typical attributes of journalistic norms, with multimedia and multiculturalism driving the change, while Thomas Hanitzsch and his colleagues examine the globally differentiated spread of normative arrangements, or Edson Tandoc and Joy Jenkins consider how events such as the *Charlie Hebdo* massacre force a rethinking of news norms. All find the norms of journalism, even in their more grounded state, to be inconsistent and contradictory to each other, so much so that, in Deuze's words, "journalism continuously reinvents itself" (2005, 447). But it does not reinvent the normative standards to which journalism repeatedly subscribes, only the grounds on which they diverge. As Deuze says about objectivity: "Objectivity may not be possible but that does not mean one should not strive for it" (448). The sticky persistence of norms wears out when the going gets tough: consider how much of the United States news media space was devoted during the Trump administration to calls for rethinking norms of objectivity, impartiality, fairness, balance, moderation, deference and the like. Yet few of those norms had changed by the end of Trump's reign, only the practical workarounds used to effect their implementation, offering at best a temporary respite from pristine ideals.

Thus, the scholarly engagement with journalism inevitably references certain occupational norms as central, and, given that they have been with journalism for close to 200 years, we might expect them to be clear-cut. Accuracy, truthfulness, accountability, independence and transparency are perhaps journalism's most readily cited normative standards, and, not surprisingly, they are heavily consonant with the western liberal democracies of late modernity. Others, less uniformly cited, include impartiality, fairness, social responsibility and service to the public good. Still others might involve deference, even-handedness and moderation. And yet others, such as objectivity, balance and neutrality, have been on their way out for decades, but are still touted in some circles. The point here is that, for all of journalism's much-proclaimed normative thinking, the precise principles that inhabit its normative imaginary are not as clear as they might be. Nor are they all necessarily relevant: what journalistic independence or news presentation looks like needs to be tailored to the context that an institution inhabits.

A triad of irrelevancies

These conditions have produced what we call a "triad of irrelevancies," an interlocking set of failed impulses that result from normative journalism's tepid and uneven reflexivity about its own positionality.

The triad of irrelevancies shows that journalistic norms have proven unthoughtful about the driving impulses of their settings of choice – the newsrooms that scattered across the liberal democratic systems of late modernity and remained in place; about the marginalized groups of such settings of choice – the women, persons of color, LGBTQIA people, indigenous populations and precarious labor forces that populate such settings without voice or agency; and about the alternatives to those settings of choice – the melded and hybrid newsrooms of the Global

South, and the internally contradictory and often anti-normative decisions that journalists there must regularly make to survive. Each part of the triad contributes to journalism's irrelevance.

Norms cater to liberal democracies

How much have journalistic norms fallen off the mark by being so stridently wedded to their settings of choice – the supposedly pristine conditions of liberal democratic newsrooms? The manifold democracies that have splintered apart on numerous continents – including Brazil, Venezuela and the United States in the Americas, Hungary, Azerbaijan and Poland in Europe, Nigeria and Kenya in Africa, Hong Kong and Malaysia in Asia, all labeled flawed democracies by *The Economist* Intelligence Unit in 2020 – are a testament that aspirational conditions are getting harder to realize on the ground.

And yet, because the norms that produce such conditions are so entrenched, journalists have been slow to call them out when they falter. Instead, as the *New Yorker*'s Jelani Cobb recently said of US journalists, the challenges of Trumpism were a "test that institutionally-minded media have by and large failed." Due to "institutional cowardice" that rendered them "slow on the uptake . . . many didn't have the temerity to anger the administration"

(2020). Equally damaging has been the naïvete with which many journalists hold on to tired and irrelevant norms, treating them like a life-vest instead of recognizing that they were already drowning, displaying, again in Cobb's words, "a stunning willingness to presume that people were acting on good faith . . . Media never got around to understanding they couldn't do things in the conventional way" (2020).

This emphasis on liberal democracy not only hides the discrepancies that occur therein, but also elides how journalists should address the issues of inequality, marginalization and oppression that plague contemporary democratic societies. It also often minimizes the other side of the binary – the work undertaken under autocratic and authoritarian regimes. Missing, then, is the ability to reach across the divide between liberal democracies and other kinds of political systems so as to identify tenable normative arrangements that might exist therein.

Norms cater to the powerful
Consider too the irrelevance of widely championed journalistic norms for those who reside in liberal democratic newsrooms but have little power. The underside of normative settings of choice does not provide an encouraging picture. The past few years

have been tumultuous for those struggling with various sources of precarity in newsrooms – gendered, racial, class, ethnic and occupational, among others – and in some cases they crystallize publicly how unempowered and disenfranchised casual labor – such as stringers or freelancers – and members of marginalized communities – such as persons of color or women – actually are. Both #BlackLivesMatter and #MeToo disrupted belief in the ability of normative standards to save journalists from irrelevance.

Just in the United States alone, multiple news organizations – a staggering list that includes almost all of the major networks, newspapers and news magazines – removed otherwise renowned journalists for misogynist and sexist behavior, while the *New York Times* remained the most visible – but not the only – newsroom to lose scores of Black journalists for troubling, and often racist, policies and coverage. When Black journalists in newsrooms within the United States are labeled biased because they bring their racialized experiences into the newsroom, it is clear that norms of optimum newsmaking are not working. Even when Wesley Lowery pointed to a "Reckoning Over Objectivity, Led by Black Journalists" in 2020, there was something discomfiting in his choice of objectivity as the frame for a much-needed point – that "the views and inclinations of whiteness" are the norm. Objectivity's failings as a concept have been so pointedly debated that the term by now should have been put to bed as an anachronism of earlier times. Its lingering presence is a testament to the sticking power of norms, regardless of their irrelevance.

Elsewhere in the Americas, seasoned reporter Maria O'Donnell posted a widely circulated tweet during the 2017 mid-term elections in Argentina that stated: "it seems that in *Clarín* no woman can provide you with the best political and economic information." Referring to an advertisement published by that country's leading daily, which claimed to offer "the best political and economic information," while featuring 12 male columnists, O'Donnell's tweet pointed to a longstanding pattern of systemic gender discrimination in Latin American newsrooms that intensifies around opinion formation: work by Eugenia Mitchelstein and her colleagues shows that 33 percent of all stories published by the 8 leading Argentine news sites two years earlier had female bylines, but that figure dropped to 15 percent when it came to opinion pieces.

Norms cater to the Global North

The normative disavowal of journalists also surfaces in alternatives to settings of choice – the

Global South. They are primarily paid heed, in line with Wendy Willems' notion of "normative dewesternization," when a southern entity "emerges from, represents the negative imprint of, or features the active intervention of the Global North" (2014, 7). Such strategic attention raises multiple issues, but key among them is how much the North has to learn from the South. Given the growing entrenchment of illiberal values, it would be useful to look toward journalists who possess "useful knowledge about how to work under hostile regimes," as James Wahutu observes about Africa.

Many conditions eliding the centers of northern normative thinking exist in acute or different forms in the Global South. Precarity, for instance, is a concept that takes on new meaning when it also involves entrenched colonialist practices, as suggested by the term "precarious professionalism," coined by Julian Matthews and Kelechi Onyemaobi (2020). Similarly, what Herman Wasserman describes as South Africa's "intensified impact of globalization with the end of the country's isolation" (2018, 81) helped to support impulses of national development that were not necessarily consonant with a northern view of norms.

The point is that, in the act of creating their own normative frameworks, journalists in the Global

South regularly strike negotiated positions with existing ones from the North. Whether it be ubuntuism in Africa or watchdog journalism in Latin America, alternative frameworks are thriving even if they have been overshadowed. In Jairo Lugo-Ocando's view, "To write its own story, journalism in the Global South needs to come to terms with the fact that the normative aspirations it upholds do not belong to her. They belong instead to an age and place where white men went to conquer, steal, rape and enslave in the name of civilization" (2020, 162).

The recognition of truly autonomous norms, built and sustained through conditions of the Global South, has been rarely acknowledged in the North. Instead, norms exist most vividly in the isolation of a global northern imaginary. As John Nerone notes, "the norms of western journalism can be inspirational, but not if treated with too much reverence" (2012, 456).

This triad of irrelevancies should give us considerable pause. It displays the extent to which normative aspirations are not serving journalists – or anyone else – as well as is claimed. Rather, by clinging to tired, partial, elitist and outdated aspirations, journalists are revealing instead not only how normatively cobbled they are but also how much of a disjuncture separates their normativity from the conditions on the ground.

Conclusion

Journalism's normative irrelevance is not a new revelation. Scholars have been saying for some time that normative arrangements can only thrive if they are consonant with the wider contexts from which journalists report and in which news organizations exist. But that is not enough anymore. Journalism is faced with a stark choice: reform or revolution. Our triad of irrelevancies shows that journalism's decline is not static, and that its potential for survival is shrinking. Journalism cannot survive without continuous questioning and tweaking by and for the collective, for, without it, norms accomplish at best vacuous, performative tasks. The result is that normative irrelevance exhausts journalists everywhere.

In an interview Ann Swidler conducted in 2013, she called on others to "look at how culture is mobilized, how it's used" in order to understand what matters: "people use culture like landmarks to orient themselves in a field of things that are possible to believe or feel or care about without absorbing any of the culture they use." She had it right: norms are landmarks of orientation, pragmatic devices for locating signposts in a map that only partially captures any given territory.

We are not the first to posit that today's unsettled times cry out for change. But we would like to be among the last. Despite the strident need for occupational norms that might help journalists out of their present turmoil, the reliance on irrelevant norms is perhaps worse than having no norms at all. It is time for journalists and journalism scholars to recognize the irrelevance of current normative configurations and do their bit to figure out which alternatives might work instead. And, if none does, perhaps it is time to rethink the value of journalistic normativity altogether. Reform or revolution? The need for change has perhaps never been greater.

4

Audiences

Widely held journalistic notions of who audiences are, and how and why they matter, currently make journalism less relevant than it ought to be. Turning our lens on audiences, we begin with two vignettes that illustrate the circumstances by which they become meaningful for the journalistic enterprise.

The first vignette took place on a cold, sunny morning in February 2008, when one of us – Boczkowski – entered the building of the American Academy of Arts and Sciences, located on a quiet, posh street near Cambridge, Massachusetts, to participate in a working group on science and the media that had brought together scientists and journalists plus the occasional media scholar. The group intended to discuss ways of informing the public more fully about scientific matters, and he had been asked to present on his emerging study of the gap between stories that news organizations consider newsworthy and stories that interest the public. During the meeting, Cornelia Dean, former editor of the Science section of the *New York Times* and currently Distinguished Lecturer and Writer-in-Residence at Brown University, shared a telling anecdote. She said that, upon being appointed editor, she had been sent to an intensive management training program, where she learned that her newspaper's marketing department had extensive data on its readers' preferences and practices, gathered through regular surveys and focus groups. But when she expressed interest in accessing those data to better plan for her section, the request was categorically denied, and she was told that knowing what readers wanted and catering to that would compromise the editorial independence of the *Times* – and, we might add, the more general aspiration of institutional autonomy in journalism.

Tellingly, this anecdote diverged markedly from a comment made during an interview that Boczkowski had conducted almost a year earlier with Fernando González, then editor of the National News Desk at *Clarín*, Argentina's highest-circulation newspaper. The interview took place in González' office in the newsroom, inside a building whose location and architecture could not contrast more with the setting of the American Academy. Nestled in the working-class neighborhood of Barracas – blocks away from Constitución, one of Buenos Aires' busiest transportation hubs – *Clarín*'s headquarters is a massive cube of cement, lacking in refinement what it symbolically exudes in economic and political power. González' office was modest – a simple desk, a few chairs, a small television set hanging on a wall opposite the desk and lots of paper sprinkled with a few family pictures. At one point during the conversation, Boczkowski asked González how much attention he paid to the online metrics of the national news stories his team wrote for the print paper. Grinning, González looked at the television set – then showing a story about Argentine tennis player Guillermo Cañas – and said:

> The only thing I pay attention to is this [grabs a piece of paper]. This is my news agenda for the day and I always write it down on the other side of the page with the ranking of the top twenty most read [stories] on Clarín.com [that was distributed and discussed at the daily morning editorial meetings]. So, I know that from today's edition . . . my cover story ranked twelfth. We have a hard time getting in [the top ten most read stories], because people are not interested, so you compete against . . . now everyone is sorry for Britney Spears . . . Cañas

makes people feel emotional nonstop [referring to the legend on the television screen, that he glances at while talking]. If I had a politician that would make people feel emotional nonstop, things would be easier for me.

The discrepancies between these two vignettes from two very different locales of contemporary journalism illustrate a seismic shift that has taken place over the past half-century regarding the role of audiences in the daily practices of mainstream journalists. The world described by Dean was one in which journalists assumed that the preferences and interests of audiences were a lesser, but not different, version of their own. Furthermore, the existence of the audience was largely assumed and taken for granted, with Dean and her colleagues presupposing that if they published good stories, readers would come to read them. The world lamented by González was one in which journalists had shifted from making assumptions about their audiences to actually knowing them. The juxtaposition between having the next day's news agenda on one side of the page and information about the news metrics from the previous day on the other embodies the then-liminal state of audiences in journalism. It also underscores the rising centrality of needing to know about audiences as part of daily newsroom rituals. What this knowledge revealed to González – consistent with the experience of many of his colleagues at his news organization and others around the globe – was that the existence of the audience could no longer be taken for granted. If journalists printed good stories, audiences might still not pay attention to them, instead of either purchasing the newspaper or coming to their news site. Uncertainty – about the fate of stories, news organizations and cumulatively journalism as a whole – became the name of the game.

This shift from assumed and taken for granted to known and uncertain audiences drives this chapter of our manifesto. Situated at the heart of the institutional disarray and growing irrelevance of contemporary journalism, it pushes us to review the circumstances underlying this shift and consider the factors that have brought about its emergence. Equally important, it prompts us to ask whether this shift can be tweaked so as to recouple journalism to the world where it belongs, in ways that might reverse, at least partly, the decoupling between the current conditions of the journalistic imagination and the conditions on the ground.

Audiences

Assumed and taken for granted audiences

During the twentieth century, the mantra repeated in newsrooms and codified in journalism textbooks around the world has been that reporters and editors at leading mainstream news organizations should cover the most newsworthy stories of the day, independently of how much audiences are interested in them. Journalism, as Herbert Gans famously put it, is about "deciding what's news." In order to make those decisions – as the work of multiple scholars has shown – reporters and editors rely on a set of norms that classify certain topics and sources as more newsworthy than others, primarily because they align with liberal democratic theory and a bureaucratized view of the world, as expressed by a narrow set of elite spokespeople. The audience is there to read, watch, listen and, ultimately, learn and be enlightened.

This has not only applied to the United States newsrooms that Gans studied in the 1960s and 1970s. Argentine reporter Carlos Ulanovsky recalls an anecdote from half a century earlier and over 10,000 kilometers south of Gans' fieldwork locations. According to Ulanovsky, when an editor of *Crítica*, a turn-of-the-century Argentine newspaper, noted that readers were "not going to like" a story that was going to print, Natalio Botana, the newspaper publisher and a seminal figure in Latin American journalism, answered that "we have to teach the public what it has to like" (2005, 97).

It is a striking cultural feat that an occupation such as journalism, whose *raison d'être* has been the pursuit of knowledge, might show a significant level of collective disinterest in what the members of the public want to know. As Robert Darnton put it when recalling his days as a reporter for the *New York Times* and the *Newark Star Ledger*, "we really wrote for one another" (1975, 176). This perception has magnified journalism's detachment from what unfolds on the ground, breeding a marked level of journalistic disengagement from actual audience preferences and practices. Instead of being known, audiences are assumed. And the assumption that audiences want to learn – or at least should learn, as Botana said – about public affairs stories, especially those that are important for the health of the body politic, only intensifies journalism's disengagement. Moreover, if audience interests are less intense than those of journalists, they are still nonetheless assumed to be consonant with each other.

This extends to specific time-worn – and worn-out – news values. For most of journalism's existence, reporters and editors in western and global northern liberal democracies have believed that audiences cherish traditional news values that accompanied most mediated public discourse in the second half of the twentieth century. Hollywood has been a predictable factory of tales to this effect – tales that have circulated globally to project an idealized and timeless image. From movies like Alan Pakula's *All the President's Men* – released in 1976 about the Watergate scandal – to Steven Spielberg's 2017 *The Post* – which narrates the story of the Pentagon Papers by inviting viewers to adopt a cultural sensibility of the 1970s – it is as if time stands still.

What this ignores is a whole set of events demonstrating evidence contradictory to what journalists would have audiences believe. In the United States alone, they have encountered the coopting of the notion of "fair and balanced" by Fox News; the botching of the story of weapons of mass destruction by the *New York Times* during the second US-led invasion of Iraq; various scandals around misrepresentation, plagiarism and lying; the lag in covering systemic racism, misogyny and xenophobia as if they mattered; the recalcitrant persistence of ethnocentrism that has treated the phenomenon of misinformation *de novo* instead of embedding it in long histories of colonialism and exploitation; and ultimately the hugely missed opportunity of reporting a more complete picture of public sentiments in the run-up to the 2016 presidential election. Although the jury is still out over coverage of the 2020 presidential election, it is fair to assume that, if things have changed, they have at best done so incrementally. In each case, instances of what Lance Bennett, Regina Lawrence and Steven Livingston (2007) aptly call "press failure" have had the singular effect of deepening the chasm between what journalists want to believe and what they refuse to see.

Worse yet, audiences have not only been assumed; they have also been taken for granted. While at the end of the twentieth century some media were still read, watched and listened to by millions of people, generating handsome advertising revenues and the reverence of political, economic and social elites, journalists and the news organizations they work for have flattened circumstances by assuming that the audience is a sure bet.

Multiple structural factors suggest otherwise, and central among them are economic concerns. The size of the audience and the regularity with which it consumed the news is more a byproduct of the natural oligopolistic position of most news organizations in their respective markets than an expression of audience interest. But, as shown by James T. Hamilton, Robert Picard and Jeffrey Brody, among others, print and audiovisual mass media require large investments and favorable regulatory conditions, creating markets with high barriers of entry, few players and large audiences. When, in the mid-1990s, the commercial web shattered both the ability to take media audiences for granted and the unstated assumption that size and presence signal a fervent yearning for the news, audiences encountered greater choice not only between news outlets but also – and perhaps more importantly – about the ability to integrate their news consumption with other forms of mediated communication, both pre-existent and emergent. In the span of a decade, the taken for granted audience was replaced by a much more uncertain one, and the prevailing assumptions about preferences and practices were being challenged by mountains of easily available data about user behavior. These data revealed that the previously held assumptions were no longer tenable – and may never have been that accurate. The question remains why it has taken so long for journalism to understand these conditions, and how its delay in doing so might affect the future sustainability of the institution.

Known and uncertain audiences

During the first half of the 1980s, the now-defunct newspaper chain Knight-Ridder – then second-largest in the United States – ran a field experiment in electronic newspapering anchored in its flagship daily, the *Miami Herald*. Viewtron, as the experiment was called, provided news, information and an array of products and services – from chat connecting consumers over the phone line to electronic commerce and servers via dedicated terminals. The first online news operation in the United States, Viewtron pioneered a number of applications that would eventually become landmark features of contemporary digital culture, but it resulted in a massive commercial failure. By the time Knight-Ridder pulled the plug, the company had allegedly lost $50 million, equivalent to over $120 million nowadays. One notable, yet rarely discussed, aspect of this initiative was that when the executives in charge looked at the server data, they found that users were far less interested in reading news stories than in chatting with other users. This crucial finding about audience behavior – which would prefigure the ascent of America Online a decade later, and social media more generally in the 2000s – was buried: with 30 percent yearly profit margins, the leadership at the chain saw no reason to stop assuming its audiences and taking them for granted.

This episode has three crucial implications for understanding key historical roots of the contemporary institutional disarray in journalism. First, one distinguishing feature between digital media and their print and audiovisual counterparts is that every act of use leaves a trace stored in the company servers. This gives editors and reporters – and their corporate bosses – granular knowledge about user behavior that is far superior to the previously existent measures of print circulation metrics, television and radio ratings, surveys and focus groups. Second, having this information does not automatically mean doing something with it. Whereas it is reasonable to speculate that any organizational decision-maker might want to utilize information of this kind to tailor the products and services provided by the organization, the Viewtron case proves that having useful information does not necessarily translate into learning effects. On the contrary, a cursory read of the financial press shows that the business landscape is littered with information neglect, especially when short-term market success brings fat bonuses and pats on the back. Third, access to this valuable information is not necessarily shared with all potentially relevant parties.

Much like the Cornelia Dean anecdote about the *New York Times*, Knight-Ridder executives did not make available the information about patterns of usage at Viewtron to editors and reporters at the *Miami Herald*, the *Philadelphia Inquirer*, the *San Jose Mercury News* or any of the other newspapers it owned at the time. We only know about it because one key Viewtron player, Roger Fidler, wrote about it in a book published in 1997, more than a decade after the project's demise.

These three implications set the stage for the dramatic shift that has taken place over the past couple of decades in how journalism as an institution views its audiences. When news organizations set up shop on the web during the second half of the 1990s, they began generating large volumes of data about audience behavior. As their commitment to digital news grew, so did its concomitant knowledge: how many pageviews each story got, how many minutes the readers spent on it, which stories they saw immediately before and after, which sites they visited immediately before and after, whether they stayed on the news site and whether they commented and/or shared the story, among others. Capturing, processing and making sense of these data became the purview of an entire cottage industry, one that included the development of new services by established players like Nielsen and the emergence of new entrants like Chartbeat. In a relatively brief period of time – especially brief if one takes a historical *longue dureé* – the audience went from being assumed to becoming known in the daily practices of newsrooms.

But this shift is not entirely due to technological innovation. Certainly, that was important, but equally important was the determination of decision-makers in the newsroom to pay attention to data about audiences. The power of this transformation in the culture of decision-making should not be underestimated: what was before either only relevant for the marketing department – and therefore off-limits to journalists because of the separation between the so-called church and state, as we saw in Dean's anecdote – or simply ignored – as we saw in the Viewtron case – now became a critical input in editorial processes. This was accompanied by another change whose cultural implications should not be missed either. Newsrooms have historically relied on highly bureaucratized top-down structures, in which relevant information is kept by a select group of decision-makers and shared with other employees on a need-to-know basis. However, in the digital world, data about audience behavior rapidly diffused across the newsroom. This included incorporating a regular review of the data into editorial meetings, as González mentioned; setting up access to basic data in the content management systems in newsrooms; and making the data visible in the workplace through mechanisms such as heat maps projected on high-definition television sets in the newsroom, or cash incentives for reporters who excelled in particular metrics. The compounding effect of these developments is not only that the audience went from assumed to known but also that ignorance became almost impossible. And yet journalistic acknowledgment has still been slow to come.

Knowing about the audience in the digital world has revealed a handful of uncomfortable facts for news organizations. First, readers do not seem massively inclined to pay for news. Even after strong marketing efforts by leading news organizations to convince their users to subscribe to their services, willingness to do so continues to be relatively low worldwide. According to Nic Newman from the Reuters Institute for the Study of Journalism at the University of Oxford, the 2020 Digital News Report shows that "across all countries most people are still not paying for online news." Second, dwindling subscription revenues have been tied to plummeting advertising revenues. Historically, advertising revenues have followed consumer attention, and the data about traffic show that this attention goes to social media and to search practices far more than to news. This is why Pew maintains that approximately 53 percent of all digital display advertising dollar revenues in the United States is collected by only two players, Facebook and Alphabet – Google's parent company. Thus, it appears that audience interest in the news might not be as strong as it was thought to be. Further bolstering this perception are studies showing that when audiences visit news sites, they pursue content that has more to do with weather, crime, sports and celebrity topics than with the national, international and economic issues which news organizations have historically seen as setting the polity's agenda.

All in all, then, knowing the audience has led to the realization that its existence has become highly uncertain. Equally important to institutional authority, knowing the audience has revealed the dismaying degree to which journalism has strayed markedly out of sync with the realities on the ground.

Recoupling audiences and journalistic practices

While the shift from assumed to known and from taken for granted to uncertain audiences has been marked by rising levels of concern in multiple corners of the journalistic world, there is a way in which it can usher in positive transformations, which would rely directly on journalistic readiness to change. Decades of assuming and taking for granted have led to a decoupling of the conditions of the imagination – how journalists conceive of their audiences as part of the editorial process – and the conditions on the ground – the actual preferences and practices of the audience. Recoupling journalism with its audiences starts from the former knowing about the latter, and from the necessarily accompanying curiosity that is tied to striving for attention rather than assuming it will always be there. Yet knowledge about audiences that is currently the coin of the realm is both extremely useful and crucially limited. It is useful because it says where the audience is at. It is limited because it does not explain why that is the case and, therefore, what else it could be.

It is helpful to view this distinction through the oft-cited lens of James W. Carey, who distinguished between communication as transmission and communication as ritual. According to him, these "two alternative conceptions of communication have been alive in American culture since this term entered common discourse in the nineteenth century" (1992 [1988], 14). Writing over 40 years ago, with a prescience that makes his ideas still highly applicable in today's much-changed media landscape, he argues that "the transmission view . . . is the commonest in our culture – perhaps in all industrial cultures – and dominates contemporary dictionary entries under the term . . . [It views] communication [a]s a process whereby messages are transmitted and distributed in space for the control of distance and people" (15). Most contemporary discussions about audiences among journalism practitioners and commentators – and also among scholars of journalism – reflect this view. They focus on metrics that quantify aspects of transmission: pageviews, time spent, shares, comments, tweets, posts and so on. The tools to capture, process and make available these metrics have evolved dramatically over the past quarter-century but, paraphrasing the iconic Led Zeppelin 1976 album and concert film, the song has remained the same. As noted above, all of this has contributed to the shift from assumed to known audiences, providing granular information about which stories capture the attention of audience members and how they interact with content on an array of digital media, including news sites, search engines and social media platforms.

It is crucial to remember that, despite the usefulness of this knowledge, it falls short of telling us why audiences behave in the ways they do. For that, we need to look at what different stories mean to them, and how these meanings relate to the incorporation of news into broader patterns of everyday life. That requires switching the gaze to a ritual view of communication, which "is directed not toward the extension of messages in space but toward the maintenance of society in time; not the act of imparting information but the representation of shared beliefs" (18). Carey adds that, "if the archetypal case of communication under a transmission view is the extension of messages across geography for the purpose of control, the archetypal case under a ritual view is the sacred ceremony that draws persons together in fellowship and commonality" (18). Thus, from a ritual view, knowledge about audiences would be less about what certain patterns in metrics reveal about the media's agenda-setting power and more about how audiences make meaning of the news from everyday conversations that build and sustain shared collective projects. These projects undergird the social lives of audiences and therefore orient their experience of, and action in, the world.

A quick glance at the content, tenor and dynamics of contemporary meaning-making processes and conversations around the news reveals that audiences appear to be more tribal, emotional, expressive and skeptical than they used to be – or at least were assumed to be – in the canonical discourse about them in both newsrooms and classrooms in the United States and other parts of the West and Global North. By tribal, we mean that today's audiences are more motivated by local contexts – kinship ties within a collective project anchored in the affirmation of a particular set of traits and/or issues – than by more impersonal ties to the polity, or an abstract greater good to be accomplished at the expense of the recognition of differences. By emotional, we underscore that current news reception practices show that interpretation is shaped by the heart as much as the mind, undercutting the primacy of dispassionate cognition as the unmarked way of making sense of the news. By expressive, we suggest that audiences are more interested in communicating about stories that matter to them and those in their local context and kinship networks and in socializing about those communicative practices than they are about dutifully listening to stories provided top-down by the news media. By skeptical, we argue that members of the audience increasingly treat trust in the news no longer as a given but as something that journalists have to earn, rendering trust a project that requires a long time to develop yet that can be undone in a hot moment.

An audience oriented to the polity and to an aspiration of rational, receptive and trustworthy exchanges has always been part and parcel of the project of modernity. The current meaning-making rituals of news audiences, however, orient to other values. Spawning practices that evolve with a regard for context, kinship, difference, emotion, expression, sociality and skepticism, today's news audiences neutralize any lingering dreams that modernity can be eternal. In order to thrive, journalism can no longer be a project of modernity and modernization, because that very project is in question.

Conclusion

The once assumed and taken for granted audience has become known and uncertain. No longer the bedrock that guaranteed news organizations handsome profits, a central place in the social imaginary and a starring role in the theatre of politics, the publics of journalism have revolted. From scrolling endlessly on social media to binge watching until dawn the latest season of a favorite thriller available on streaming platforms, large segments of the audiences are gravitating to alternative forms of content and therefore eroding the once-stable bedrock of attention – and its accompanying revenue. Moreover, tribal, emotional, expressive and skeptical practices undercut the tenets of the golden age of mainstream news and its modern ethos in ways that further compromise its sustainability.

What is journalism to do? Standing still seems a sure recipe for extinction. The dilemma is, as with issues of elites and norms, whether the institution embarks on a reformist survival project or attempts a revolutionary overhaul. To these alternative pathways we devote the next and last chapter of this manifesto.

5

Reform or Revolution?

We have stated variously throughout this manifesto that journalism is at a crossroads: if it is to recouple itself with the larger society in which it is embedded and offset its growing irrelevance in the twenty-first century, it must embrace either a reformist path or a revolutionary path. While a combination of both paths might be possible under certain circumstances, their contours are sufficiently different for them to merit separate treatment.

The reformist path

We should start by emphasizing that, for many journalists, reform will not be easy. Indeed, in some cases, it may even be harder to imagine than revolution, insofar as it attempts to work with already existing materials and grow them in new directions. At the root of the reformist path is what we think of as a movement from a tacit to an explicit democratic liberalism that emphasizes transformative action as journalism's guiding *raison d'être*. In each of the institutional interfaces we have outlined so far – journalism's relationship with elites, norms and audiences – we have argued that a major problem with contemporary journalism is that it takes certain aspects of its existence for granted, seeing cases and conditions as permanent states of affairs rather than as contingent adaptations that can evolve if the situation demands it. One of the most prevalent aspects of journalism, as it evolved in the Global North and insofar as its rhetoric has penetrated the imagined conditions of journalism elsewhere, is its fundamental liberal democratic political orientation. This orientation is so basic and prevalent that it has usually been ignored or forgotten, except in moments of extreme crisis or conflict. Adopting a path toward reform would involve moving from an implicit democratic liberalism to an inclusive and equitable democratic liberalism that foregrounds transformation as the core of journalism's understanding of what it is for.

Take, first, journalism's relationship to elites. Embedded in journalism's imaginary has been the notion – often complex and contradictory – that journalism simultaneously acts as a check on elite behavior, often in lieu of the citizenry, and yet relies on elites for much of its information, as well as its political authority. As already noted, changes in journalism in some countries over the past decade have largely stemmed from what we call the crack up of the elites, whereby the anti-liberal tendencies of some elites in once-staid liberal democracies have laid bare the underlying liberal orientation of much of the political media. This has forced the latter to choose between their values and what they see as their duty to report about those in positions of political power. In some cases, one outcome has been that journalists are increasingly caught between a tacit democratic liberalism – one that is taken for granted and rarely expressed because it is the default position – and complications of that liberalism that are aired verbally as core journalistic principles, but not often enacted in practice: "there are not two sides to every debate" or "leaders should be criticized for anti-liberal behavior even if they are democratically elected."

If pushed toward reform, journalism, to some degree, would still prioritize processes of governance, but they would be rooted in a respect for alternative points of view and for the other side of the political argument, rather than the processes of electoral democracy only. If elites violated these basic liberal norms, they would be called out for their actions by journalists. A reformist path would see this arrangement as the continuation of a force-fully expressed and articulate democratic realism, even under conditions where political life seems to have returned to something akin to normal. Journalism's first allegiance would be to liberal, democratic governance, even under conditions in which democratically elected leaders act in anti-liberal ways – and journalists would state so readily.

Though this would be a major change in journal-istic rhetoric and practice, it would not be enough on its own to constitute much of a reform. Instead, the open embrace of a liberal position would allow journalists to begin the hard work of thinking about the processes of inclusion and exclusion that have undergirded the modern democratic project. Who is counted as a legitimate constituency in liberal democratic processes, and who is left out? As we hope to have shown in this manifesto, the excluded are usually communities that have been historically marginalized and oppressed, and the elites of these communities have been left out of the picture as well. Alongside a redoubled commitment to liberal-ism would come a profound attempt to broaden the circles of elite representation, so that democracy might work for a greater number and kind of constituencies than it has served or reflected thus far. In other words, the elites that journalism would prioritize would no longer be high-status elites, but those representing the voices of historically disenfranchised groups, thus expanding the set of voices, concerns and frameworks in the news. Elite membership in the journalistic pantheon would be both more open and subject to higher and more equitable standards.

This discussion of taken-for-grantedness takes us to our next area of concern, the role that norms play in the operation of journalistic institutions. For a useful reform of journalistic norms, we argue that journalists must refocus their normative orientation to address the triad of irrelevancies identified in chapter 3: overcoming their narrow definitions of "who counts" in order to go beyond the powerful in liberal democracies of the Global North. To reach such an end, journalists would need to embrace alternative norms of inclusiveness, social justice and cosmopolitanism.

The alternative norm of inclusiveness would require reporters and editors to strive toward inclusion in the stories they tell, the frames they choose and the sources they include. By inclusiveness, we mean a journalism that gives voices to the wide array of peoples who constitute contemporary society, in all of their diversity and without flattening their complexity. This is a far cry from the worldview that Mark Fishman uncovered in 1980 in relation to journalism being bureaucratically organized, since vast swaths of society – especially the more marginalized and oppressed – were excluded from his target population. Our notion of inclusiveness necessarily involves the marginalized and oppressed, whose lack of visibility and organization is part and parcel of what disenfranchises them. A journalism of inclusion would seek to make visible precisely what the normative structures of traditional, mainstream reporting routinely push from view.

Building on the dynamics of inclusion, a reformed journalism might also take up social justice as an essential norm of the twenty-first century. Paraphrasing Gregory Bateson's definition of information as "a difference which makes a difference" (1972, 465), a journalism embracing social justice is one in which the ultimate goal would be to share information that makes a difference in the living conditions of those who, as noted above, have historically less of a chance to make a difference on their own. In other words, rather than reporting on all the news that's fit to print, a norm of social justice would prioritize reporting all the news that makes a difference, turning media institutions into platforms for reform rather than for the maintenance of a status quo that has long turned a blind eye to systemic forms of injustice.

Journalists also would embrace cosmopolitanism as an occupational norm, in the best and most noble sense of that much maligned word. By cosmopolitanism, we are not arguing for a faceless, capital-driven globalization that really serves as a mask for American corporate interests; nor do we mean a type of journalism that serves only placeless people. What we mean is a journalism that is curious about how news gets made in places that might initially seem strange or far away, particularly those in the Global South; a journalism that does not try to imagine that there is only one right or best way to do things; and a journalism that learns about and adopts practices that might serve today's political conditions, rather than remain indebted to the outdated norms of the past. A cosmopolitan reform of journalistic norms would embrace and learn from difference, both within nations and across them.

Finally, to reform its relationships with audiences, we argue that journalism has to meet them where they are, rather than where it would like them to be. It has to engage their contemporary rituals around the news instead of pretending they will abandon them to merely absorb information. It has to stretch to accommodate audiences that may fit few of the contours most prized in now inert assumptions of public engagement. It has to tell stories that appeal to interpretations from the heart as much as from the mind, instead of continuing to provide dispassionate accounts of events because that is what objectivity in the news is supposed to be about. It has to acknowledge differences in lived experience and articulate recognition as the foundational social bond of context and kinship networks, instead of prioritizing the impersonal ideals of a polity that has long favored certain communities at the expense of others in the name of a greater good.

We have discussed what a sea change it would be for journalists to take their audiences more seriously than they do now. In part, this stems from the fact that much of journalism in the twentieth century saw the essence of "professionalism" as maintaining a dynamic distance from audiences, allowing journalists to deliberately not take outsider preferences into account. Audiences were the "clients" of journalists, and like any other client in a professional relationship, they did not know what they wanted or what was good for them. It was the journalists' job to give them the information they needed, not the information they thought they desired.

How can journalistic professionalism survive if audiences suddenly have agency? Will the very idea of journalism as a professional category fade away? Under the reformist path we outline here, this need not be the case. Part of the confusion stems from a client-based model of professional understanding, one that tries to imitate the venerable professions of medicine and law. But other professions do not preach or talk down to their audiences – musicians and artists, for one, as well as other workers classified as creatives. Perhaps journalists ought to start thinking of themselves less like lawyers or doctors and more like jazz musicians, actors, dancers or visual artists. No jazz musician would ever say that they do not take their audience into account when they perform. But this does not make them any less professional. Perhaps it would be beneficial to start thinking of journalism this way, too.

Ultimately, in such a reconstituted connection with its audiences, journalism has to seek out the kinds of transformation that will support social justice, the bedrock from which trust is earned. It must do so instead of pursuing abstract values that under the veneer of fairness have led to the rising distrust of a once venerable institution and the dreams of the project of modernity writ large. To foster social justice, a reformed relationship with audiences should center on portraying injustices as systemic phenomena instead of episodic situations, foregrounding the underlying conditions that lead to inequities and inquiring into concrete ways of modifying them rather than merely witnessing their occurrence.

The revolutionary path

A second alternative also awaits consideration. For, at the same time as we see value in journalism's reform, there is a seduction in bypassing the incremental steps necessary for reform to pivot us in another direction – toward revolution. Though contemporary institutions do not readily embrace even notions of non-violent revolution – Ralph Waldo Emerson (1967 [1841], n.p.) once admitted how ashamed he was that people readily hung on to and "capitulate[d] to badges and names, large societies and dead institutions" – the continued relevance of journalism might lie in the promise of a no-holds-barred makeover.

If the central impulse of the reformist path is moving from tacit to explicit, and from exclusionary to inclusive democratic liberalism, then the path to revolution is about taking the many hidden dimensions and offshoots of democratic liberalism that clutter journalism's imaginary and turning them loose to the world. Although democratic liberalism has long fueled unmarked assumptions about what good journalism could look like, a revolutionary view holds it responsible for much of journalism's unnecessarily narrowed positionality. As the sentiment goes, democracy needs journalism to survive, but journalism proliferates in many forms without the aid of democracy, of the liberal or illiberal sort.

Challenging the default assumptions of democratic liberalism invites in its stead other kinds of emancipatory political arrangements to the table. Their involvement, reflecting multiple sets of journalistic practices on the ground, ends up mixing into journalism's operation various kinds of practices in situations of anti-authoritarianism, tentative steps toward democratization, creative acts of resistance that bear little similarity to current aspirations for newswork, workarounds to settler-colonialism, and so on and so forth. When different sets of practices are incorporated as part of the conditions that necessarily foster a fuller repertoire than those heralded by a liberal democratic mindset, we might find an occupational landscape that is energized by its fight against practices of censorship, impunity, corruption and collusion, on the one hand, and against racism, homophobia, sexism, misogyny, classism and other strands of oppression, on the other. Across the board of possibilities, the practices of journalism on the ground land far from the aspirational imaginary attached to democratic liberalism. Yet such practices already live everywhere in the world, and it is through that world that journalism needs to find its path forward to relevance.

Makeovers are a useful metaphor here because they offer the chance to begin anew without having to think through all the details of what has gone awry or why revolution has suddenly become an enticing fix. How democratic liberalism turned into part of the journalistic endeavor should not be the center of attention right now; instead, what concerns us is recoupling journalism's relevance in the here-and-now. Each of our institutional interfaces – elites, norms and audiences, as acted upon by journalists – provides a different, but interconnected, specter of how to imagine an alternative future grounded not in institutional interfaces that take us back to democratic liberalism, but in the practices of newsmaking on the ground, practices that exist no matter how much or how little democracy and liberalism are there for the taking.

If we pivot toward revolution as the end move of journalism's reset, journalists need to rid themselves of their reliance on elites, throw out their regard for norms and challenge their differentiation from audiences. In other words, embracing revolution requires eradicating all those terms that have been crafted to prevent it from happening. A liberal democratic mindset – and the elites, norms and audiences that drive it – ensures that a tempered institutional sensibility follows. But if revolution is to succeed, elites, norms and audiences must go. In their place, journalists must develop a keener understanding of their own practices and how they can be used for radical transformation.

To elites, first. Revolting against elites calls for a fuller recognition of their failings, which might weigh heavily on any value they still have. Elites sometimes exist because others allow them to. Societies, groups, organizations and even individuals routinely and ritualistically recognize their status and power, bequeathing them ongoing regard so long as they play to rule. But they are more unstable than they appear. Consider Meghan Markle's recent denunciation of the symbiotic link between the tabloids in the United Kingdom and the British Royal Family. Not only did her push-back unsettle longstanding modes of decorum around the monarchy, and journalism's role in sustaining it regardless of consequence, but it also displayed how inexpert, strategic and fundamentally distasteful were the conversations, actions and decision-making displayed by the elites involved.

What if journalism were to challenge the authority of elites and proclaim them irrelevant? Design workarounds to bring about their erasure? Supplant them with arrangements that fulfill their roles better than they do? If the reformist path has us developing mechanisms to include more fully the elites of the historically disenfranchised and marginalized, the revolutionary path adds to that an injunction to imagine a journalism without elites at all.

A horizon without elites has the capacity to offer journalists, sources and audiences a more equitable and direct relationship with each other. Indeed, the very idea of doing away with elites is woven into much of the scholarship in journalism studies, foreshadowed by the technological advancements that have helped to characterize newsmaking, and invited by the powerful impulses associated with social justice movements and their impact on what matters as news.

The erasure of elites must begin with journalists themselves. Spreading the riches equitably among the press corps, however limited they might be, would go a long way toward effacing the multiple layers of precarity that plague newsrooms today: internal racism, classism, sexism and gender bias, settler-colonialism, ethnocentrism and short-term casual labor are but a few of the biases and inequities that need supplanting. We might finally see solidarity in newsrooms, and shared pacts for disrupting all kinds of risks and intimidation. Without elites in the newsroom, we might be more inclined to imagine and accommodate inclusive, equitable and diverse conditions for conducting and accessing newswork. When a recent audit of the *Philadelphia Inquirer*, conducted by Temple University researchers to assess the paper's problematic diversity and inclusiveness, found an alarming correspondence between elites acting as sources and a consequent lack of diversity in the newsroom and news content, barely a response was heard across journalistic circles in the United States. The reset would repeat itself with sources, whereby protesters on the ground would have as much voice as the police officers who constrain them, if not more; and with publics, where the imagined construct of news users would be as fully diverse as the publics themselves.

Like elites, norms too would be booted out the door in a revolutionary turn. Imagine a news environment that is not hampered by moderation, balance or objectivity. Does it sound far-fetched? It should not, for in many views we are already there. But we need to own it to make it matter. Consider the stridency with which liberal and illiberal forces regularly and systematically eviscerate each other in multiple places around the globe – all in the name of norms. This produces a frenzied reliance on norms believed to be still present rather than a move toward alternative values. The delayed journalistic push-back to presidential press conferences under the Trump administration is a case in point. When Donald Trump revealed in 2016 that he had less interest in letting the rituals of the press conference play out than in demeaning reporters who attended, journalists in the United States hung on long past the ritual's usefulness. In such cases, journalistic norms rear their head more like an emblem of atrophy than a lever for change. Their entrenchment in democratic liberalism gives them value that is desired but sorely matched to ground conditions.

For norms can only play to the least normatively inclined player. Thus, an environment without norms necessitates the development of an alternative means for assessing journalism which is in conference with what is doable rather than imaginable. If cobbled practices are what we have in hand, then they – not normative standards – are what needs to guide action. Otherwise, as we see today, the gap between norms and practices will continue to expand, making norms both increasingly abstract and deeply entrenched. Conflict reporting, for example, would replace the oft-heralded aims of balance or impartiality in the journalism of wartime with guides to better practice: training in trauma and loss, workarounds for anxiety and depression, guidelines for sustaining physical endurance, the development of detailed insurance arrangements or safety protocols for multiple kinds of contingencies. For a reporter staring down the barrel of a gun, how much does objectivity matter? How relevant is decorum if a photographer needs to scramble for water, food and housing? The provision of practical hints about how to gauge the dangerous situations of conflict zones has far more relevance for journalists – and journalism – than the settling-in of abstract and often unattainable normative cues.

Without norms to repeatedly remind journalists of what they ought to be when they put on their journalistic attire, journalists might find themselves in a more direct linkage with the events, issues and people that drew them to newsmaking to begin with. Other cues of practice, many of them forgotten, might take the place of receding norms, with journalists freed up to address impulses of curiosity, improvisation, exploration and resourcefulness that we know often help to orient budding reporters to occupational identities but fade the longer journalists act as journalists. Without the constraints created by norms, these initial values about the craft of newswork might be recaptured and migrate to the front stages of occupational mindsets. Getting real about the real conditions of reporting means letting go of norms as currently conceived and typically enacted.

A revolutionary view of norms reminds us that some of the best journalistic work surfaces precisely when journalists do not do what they ought to or should do, but when they challenge this at its core: think Watergate in the United States, environmental justice reportage in Asia and Latin America, and the Panama Papers that resulted in collaborations among journalists in 80 countries. A journalism without norms might entice journalists to venture excitedly across an as-yet untraveled terrain. Given that journalism has always been at least partly about mavericks, when did going rogue get such a bad name in newsmaking?

Like elites and norms, audiences also need to be shunted from the picture. Implying a differentiation between those who create and those who consume or use the news, by definition audiences create an "other." And though recent developments in journalism have been increasingly accommodating audiences with more extensive degrees of participation in newsmaking, each choice still hinges on a fundamental differentiation between newsmakers and news users.

Losing that differentiation might enable journalists to finally take back their places in their communities of choice, helping them to work journalistically as members of those communities. Were the notion of audiences to be absorbed, journalists might finally find a way to speak on behalf of a community driven by best interests, passions, local concerns and future visions. By reattaching journalists to communities rather than fostering their separation, the promise of new forms of attachment might help to generate a redefinition of newsmaking as inextricably tied to the communities it serves.

Although losing the audience might appear too radical in today's world of highly bureaucratized journalism, its promise is far from unrecognized. On September 24, 1690, Benjamin Harris published the inaugural issue of *Publick Occurrences, Both Forreign and Domestick* in Boston, Massachusetts; it was also the last issue as the colonial rulers prohibited Harris from continuing with his newspaper since he did not have their authorization. The issue consisted of four pages but had the peculiar feature that only three of them had news content. Harris left the fourth page intentionally blank. Appreciating that people would read the newspaper and pass it around the community, he wanted the fourth page to become the place where readers would contribute their news and opinion. This would endow the content of the newspaper with an organic quality and lessen the separation between the printer and the readers. The newspaper, in other words, would become a communal artifact, written for and in no small measure by the community.

Revolution, then, pushes us to leap into the somewhat murky, but by no means total, unknown. Perhaps its proposal seems radical. Or perhaps today's revolution in journalism begins to envision the future by going back to the past.

Towards a journalism that matters

Going back to the past is an act of many guises. Kurt Vonnegut, Jr.'s novel *Slaughterhouse-Five* begins with this famous opening line: "Listen: Billy Pilgrim has come unstuck in time." In Vonnegut's sobering tale of World War II and its aftermath, Billy Pilgrim may travel through time but his past,

present and future are unchangeable. Some inter-
pret time travel in *Slaughterhouse-Five* as little more
than a cruel trick played by an alien intelligence,
wherein the various fates and tragedies that await
the novel's characters loom large no matter how
anyone attempts to change the outcome.

Others, though, see Billy Pilgrim's relationship
with time as an immobilizing experience of trauma,
one that takes time out of sequence and forces a
small set of actions to be enacted over and over,
regardless of how mundane, inappropriate, unpro-
ductive or constraining their repetition might be.
Trauma is one way of visiting the past that leaves
residue on whatever it touches. Because that residue is temporally crafted – simultaneously pinning
its subjects to the time of the traumatic experience
while pushing away other points in time from view
– it threatens to loosen one's grip of what exists
on the ground. Coming "unstuck" in time, then, is
another way of underscoring an ungrounded life,
an existence in the clouds, an unreal reality driven
heavily by the imagination.

Journalism today is unstuck in time, its existence
undermined by its decoupling of the conditions of
the imagination from the conditions on the ground.
This manifesto has shown how it mindlessly repeats
the mantras of days gone by, even though falling

back onto seemingly obvious solutions satisfies little more than base impulses of familiarity. In the best of times, such mantras have scant impact on facilitating change for and among journalists. But in the worst of times, when change is necessary for the survival of the journalistic institution, they fall way short of orienting journalism toward the transformation it so sorely needs.

Like the time-traveling main character in Vonnegut's tale, we have argued in this manifesto that journalism's unstuckness – its decoupling from the ground conditions that fuel longstanding modes of interfacing with elites, norms and audiences – has caused journalists to lose their compass about what truly matters. Journalism finds itself less socially, politically and culturally relevant than it ought to be, and certainly less relevant than it thinks it is. It also finds itself in circumstances that invite a rethinking of where it has gone wrong and how it might proceed differently – if only journalists would think to look.

Perhaps this is as it should be. For from the earliest days of trauma's reckoning, there has always been a map toward its cure. When Freud bore down on repetition as the tool by which to move out of trauma and toward recovery, he might have been offering a light to journalism's eventual transformation. Though it is not always the case, the consequences of trauma can be accommodated, mitigated and sometimes controlled. But, to get to that point, they require first to be recognized, named and understood.

Transformation may thus be upon us, if journalism can only recognize, name and understand why it has arrived at its current crisis and what its eventual resolution might involve. Throughout this chapter, we have tried to highlight both reformist and revolutionary strategies that can help journalism to regain its political and social resonance in contemporary settings. Recoupling or – in Vonnegut's more evocative term – stuckness may be journalism's way out. This manifesto shows how journalism might indeed get stuck yet again, gripped enough by the here-and-now to finally let go of what should have been retired long ago. It is our hope that the possible pathways we have detailed here may help journalists to realize a more just world for everyone, but especially for those marginalized communities who have long read, watched and listened to the news from the sidelines.

And so it goes.

Bibliography

Askanias, Tina and Hartley, Jannie Moller (2019, September). "Framing Gender Justice: A Comparative Analysis of the Media Coverage of #MeToo in Denmark and Sweden," *Nordicom Review* 40 (2), 19–36.

Bateson, Gregory (1972). *Steps to an Ecology of Mind*. New York: Chandler Publishing Company.

Bennett, W. Lance (1990). "Toward a Theory of Press–State Relations in the United States," *Journal of Communication* (Spring 1990), 103–25.

Bennett, W. Lance, Lawrence, Regina and Livingston, Steven (2007). *When the Press Fails: Political Power and the News Media from Iraq to Katrina*. University of Chicago Press.

Callison, Candis and Young, Mary Lynn (2020). *Reckoning: Journalism's Limits and Possibilities*. New York: Oxford University Press.

Carey, James W. (1992 [1988]). *Communication as*

Culture: Essays on Media and Society. New York: Routledge.

Cobb, Jelani (2020, December 4). Conference remarks given at "Black Media Makers and the Fierce Urgency of Now," Annenberg School for Communication at the University of Pennsylvania, Philadelphia.

Colyvas, Jeannette and Powell, Walter (2006). "Roads to Institutionalization," *Research in Organizational Behavior* 27, 305–53.

Connell, Raewyn (2002). *Gender*. Cambridge: Polity.

Coronel, Sheila (2020, June 16). "This Is How Democracy Dies," *The Atlantic*: www.theatlantic.com/interna tional/archive/2020/06/maria-ressa-rappler-philippin es-democracy/613102.

Crouse, Timothy (1973). *The Boys on the Bus*. New York: Random House.

Crowley, Michael, Jakes, Lara and Sander, David E. (2019, November 9). "How the State Dept.'s Dissenters Incited a Revolt, Then a Rallying Cry," *The New York Times*: www.nytimes.com/2019/11/09/us/ politics/impeachment-state-department.html.

Darnton, Robert (1975). "Writing News and Telling Stories," *Daedalus* 104 (2), 175–94.

Deuze, Mark (2005, November). "What Is Journalism? Professional Identity and Ideology of Journalists Reconsidered," *Journalism: Theory, Practice and Criticism* 6 (4), 442–64.

Bibliography

Durkheim, Émile (1982 [1893]). *The Division of Labor in Society*. New York: The Free Press.

Durkheim, Émile (2014 [1895]). *The Rules of Sociological Method*. New York: Simon and Schuster.

Economist Intelligence Unit, *The* (2020). "Democracy Index 2020: In Sickness and In Health": www.eiu.com/n/campaigns/democracy-index-2020.

Emerson, Ralph Waldo (1967 [1841]). *Self-Reliance*. White Plains, NY: Peter Pauper Press.

Fidler, Roger (1997). *Mediamorphosis: Understanding New Media*. Thousand Oaks, CA: Pine Forge Press.

Fishman, Mark (1980). *Manufacturing the News*. Austin: University of Texas Press.

Fourie, Pieter J. (2008). "Ubuntuism as a Framework for South African Media Practice and Performance: Can It Work?" *Communicatio* 34 (1), 53–79.

Freud, Sigmund (1958 [1914]). "Remembering, Repeating and Working Through," in James Strachey (ed.), *The Standard Edition of the Complete Psychological Works of Sigmund Freud* (Vol. XII). London: Hogarth Press, 145–56.

Gans, Herbert (1979). *Deciding What's News: A Study of CBS Evening News, NBC Nightly News, Newsweek, and Time*. New York: Random House.

George, Cherian (2016). *Hate Spin*. Cambridge, MA: The MIT Press.

Giddens, Anthony (1984). *The Constitution of Society*. Cambridge: Polity.

Bibliography

Goffman, Erving (1955). "On Face-Work: An Analysis of Ritual Elements in Social Interaction," *Psychiatry: Journal for the Study of Interpersonal Processes* 18, 213–31.

Hall, Stuart (1973). "The 'Structured Communication' of Events" (discussion paper). University of Birmingham: www.birmingham.ac.uk/Documents/college-artslaw/history/cccs/stencilled-occasional-papers/1to8and11to24and38to48/SOP05.pdf.

Hallett, Tim and Ventresca, Marc J. (2006, April). "Inhabited Institutions: Social Interactions and Organizational Forms in Gouldner's *Patterns of Industrial Bureaucracy*," *Theory and Society* 35 (2), 213–26.

Hallin, Daniel (1989). *The Uncensored War: The Media and Vietnam*. Berkeley: University of California Press.

Hamilton, James T. (2004). *All the News That's Fit to Sell*. Princeton University Press.

Hanitzsch, Thomas, Hanusch, Folker, Ramaprasad, Jyotika and de Beer, Arnold S. (2019). *Worlds of Journalism: Journalistic Cultures Around the Globe*. New York: Columbia University Press.

Hughes, Everett C. (1936, April). "The Ecological Aspect of Institutions," *American Sociological Review* 1 (2), 180–9.

Jackson, Sarah J. (2018). *Black Celebrity, Racial Politics and the Press*. New York: Routledge.

Bibliography

Kovach, Bill and Rosenstiel, Tom (2014 [2001]). *The Elements of Journalism* (3rd edition). New York: Three Rivers Press.

Lippmann, Walter (1922). *Public Opinion*. New York: Harcourt, Brace and Co.

Lowery, Wesley (2020, June 23). "A Reckoning Over Objectivity, Led by Black Journalists," *The New York Times*: www.nytimes.com/2020/06/23/opinion/objectivity-black-journalists-coronavirus.html.

Lugo-Ocando, Jairo (2020). *Foreign Aid and Journalism in the Global South*. London: Lexington Books.

Mabogunje, Akin L. (2000, December 5). "Institutional Radicalization, the State, and the Development Process in Africa," *PNAS* 97 (25), 14007–14.

Matthews, Julian and Onyemaobi, Kelechi (2020). "Precarious Professionalism: Journalism and the Fragility of Professional Practice in the Global South," *Journalism Studies* 21 (13), 1836–51.

Mellado, Claudia (ed.) (2020). *Beyond Journalistic Norms*. London: Routledge.

Mitchelstein, E., Boczkowski, Pablo and Andelsman, Victoria (2019). "Whose Voices are Heard? The Byline Gender Gap on Argentine News Sites," *Journalism: Theory, Practice and Criticism*: https://journals.sagepub.com/doi/10.1177/1464884919848183.

Monroe, Bryan and Wentzel, Andrea (2021, February 12). *The Philadelphia Inquirer 2020 Diversity and Inclusion Audit*. Philadelphia, PA: Temple University Klein

Bibliography

College of Media and Communication: https://drive. google.com/file/d/1MJB8IaP4MC_kpP47ZGsVo5y1c AR3VByR/view.

Nerone, John (2012). "The Historical Roots of the Normative Model of Journalism," *Journalism: Theory, Practice and Criticism* 14 (4), 446–58.

Newman, Nic (2020). *Executive Summary and Key Findings of the 2020 Report*. Reuters Institute for the Study of Journalism: www.digitalnewsreport.org/ survey/2020/overview-key-findings-2020.

Parsons, Talcott (1951). *The Social System*. Glencoe, IL: The Free Press.

Pew Research Center (2020, July 14). "About Half of All Digital Display Advertising Revenue Goes to Facebook, Google": www.pewresearch.org/ft_20-07-10_digitalnative_feature_new.

Picard, Robert and Brody, Jeffrey (1997). *The Newspaper Publishing Industry*. Boston: Allyn & Bacon.

Reese, Stephen D. (2021). *The Crisis of the Institutional Press*. Cambridge: Polity.

Searle, John (1969). *Speech Acts*. Cambridge University Press.

Siavelis, Peter (2016). "Crisis of Representation in Chile? The Institutional Connection," *Journal of Politics in Latin America* 8 (3), 61–93.

Simmel, Georg (1955). *Conflict and the Web of Group Affiliations*. New York: The Free Press.

Squires, Catherine R. (2014). *The Post-Racial Mystique:*

Bibliography

Media and Race in the Twenty-First Century. NYU Press.

Swidler, Ann (1986, April). "Culture in Action: Symbols and Strategies," *American Sociological Review* 51 (2), 273–86.

Swidler, Ann (2013, August 22). YouTube interview, University of California at Berkeley, Sociology: www.youtube.com/watch?v=8Oc7adxa1_w.

Tandoc, Edson and Jenkins, Joy (2017, August). "Journalism Under Attack: The *Charlie Hebdo* Covers and Reconsiderations of Journalistic Norms," *Journalism: Theory, Practice and Criticism* 20 (9), 1165–82.

Taylor, Charles (2004). *Modern Social Imaginaries*. Durham, NC: Duke University Press.

Tuchman, Gaye (1978). *Making News*. New York: The Free Press.

Ulanovsky, Carlos (2005). *Paren las rotativas: Diarios, revistas y periodistas (1920–1969)*. Buenos Aires: Emece.

Vonnegut, Jr., Kurt (1969). *Slaughterhouse-Five, or the Children's Crusade*. New York: Delacorte Press.

Wahutu, James (2019). "Western Journalists, Learn from Your African Peers," NiemanLab Predictions for Journalism 2020: www.niemanlab.org/2019/12/western-journalists-learn-from-your-african-peers.

Waisbord, Silvio (2000). *Watchdog Journalism in South America*. New York: Columbia University Press.

Bibliography

Waisbord, Silvio (2013). *Reinventing Professionalism.* Cambridge: Polity.

Wasserman, Herman (2018). *Media, Geopolitics, and Power.* Bloomington: Indiana University Press.

Weber, Max (1968 [1922]). "Bureaucracy," in *Economy and Society.* New York: Bedminster Press, 956–1005.

Willems, Wendy (2014). "Beyond Normative Dewesternization: Examining Media Culture from the Vantage Point of the Global South," *The Global South* 8 (1), 7–23.

Williams, Raymond (1976). *Keywords.* Oxford University Press.